Reflections of the Heart

Writings from Sacred Center

with

Lyn Holley Doucet

Library of Congress Control Number: 2011901177
ISBN: Hardcover   978-1-4568-5818-6
                 Softcover   978-1-4568-5817-9
                 eBook   978-1-4568-5819-3

Print information available on the last page.

Rev. date: 09/20/2018

To order additional copies of this book, contact:
Xlibris
1-888-795-4274
www.Xlibris.com
Orders@Xlibris.com
532608

CONTENTS

About the Cover Art

While preparing an Advent prayer service for a women's prayer group, I was inspired to paint **Mary Dancing Among the Stars** after reading a poem by Macrina Wiederkehr, OSB, from the book **A Tree Full of Angels, Seeking the Holy in the Ordinary.** There is a line in the poem,

> "You came as a star
> led by a star
> through the stars
> to the stars
> We never knew we were stars
> until you came."

These words compelled me to paint and the result was the image that became the cover art for this book. Mary is a model of hopefulness and rejoicing even in the most unlikely and unexpected of circumstances. It is my thought that the collected writings in this book will give one breathing space, a space to realign, to allow something to grow within, to keep hope in the heart, rejoice even in the most unlikely of circumstances, and to know that we are stars.

—Trudy Gomez

Introduction

Photo by Wendi Romero

When the Soul wants to experience something, she throws out an image in front of her then steps into it.
—*Meister Eckhart*

Sacred Center was birthed when I decided to sit in centering prayer for thirty minutes each Thursday morning. I sent an invitation to any who might want to join me. And such beautiful souls responded. Whether we were sharing the deepest hurts or longings of the heart, or sitting silently in prayer, the bonds between us grew tight and strong, and we became sisters. We are mothers, artists, grandmothers, caregivers, poets, writers, and teachers. Our ages and experiences vary. We are many things, but we know these are just our roles. Our essence lies in our quest as spiritual seekers and lovers of Spirit. Our identity is held in the mind of God. As the author of A Cloud of Unknowing tells us, "Not what I am but that I am, not what God is but that he is."

The deep hunger for the experience of God is the power that brought Sacred Center into being. I believe that this group is a miracle because it wasn't planned and couldn't even be completely visualized. It manifested itself out of the profound longing of the heart for what is real, sacred, and lasting. This is what brings women together in a little cabin in Maurice, Louisiana.

It is amazing to me, even now, that so many soulful women, busy as women always are, gather once a week to sit in silence and contemplation. We hold a belief that the language of God is silence, and God might move in silent and magnificent ways when we calm down, embrace quiet, and open our hearts. We offer one another support to live in a way that is alien to many: the walking of the contemplative path. We ask nothing of one another but a shared presence.

At Sacred Center, we have found complete acceptance as we are. Here, no one seeks to change us or mold our thoughts. We believe that each one of us has everything she needs within her, like gold buried deeply in the soul. Practices of contemplation help us access the gold that has been there all along.

I gathered some quotes from members who tell us what Sacred Center means to them.

Deidre Montgomery: The center provides a space for me to share my heart thoughts without judgment or disbelief. It is that soft cushion on which to land when I fall, or the explosion of laughter in the reality of what is. It is a place where I can show up just as I am, wherever I am, and know the love that is beyond all measurement. No one claims to know the answers, but it is certainly enlightening to ask the questions. We each live into our individual knowing. That's just a taste of my experience; the rest is ineffable.

Dana Manly: Who are we as spiritual sisters? We are seekers who guide one another through our presence and deep listening. Some days are more challenging than others; we bring our whole selves to the moment—full of aggravation, frustration, and the need to be heard, loved, and embraced with all our warts. We bring our peace, gratitude, abundance, love, and grace. We make all parts one whole. Unity, oneness, a Sacred Circle, a Sacred Center that we carry within us as we walk our path(s) in the world.

Avis Lyons: Divine guidance brought me here; divine thirst and love keep me coming. The women of Sacred Center express such a great collection of wisdom that life gets bigger and bigger from my knowing them. I am so awed by the thoughts and observations of these beautiful spirits that I continue to seek a seat in the company of these guides who don't guide and spiritual directors who don't direct; their guidance comes from being women living the most authentically they can in the moment, very often with a burst of laughter!

Trudy Gomez: Sacred Center is about holding space. That is what sacred center does, allows us to hold space for one another, to be loved and love without fear, without judgment, to be authentically ourselves.

Jan Menard: Sacred Center is a place where God is present for each of us. Also present within our midst are joy, freedom, and serenity.

For me, the presence of the Holy Spirit is palpable, propping us up when needed and celebrating with us as we come closer to our understanding of ourselves and our Lord.

Pat Low: I woke in the middle of the night with this thought: Words cannot describe the silence. We show up, and grace fills our empty spaces.

Lissee Spiller: It's a place where I can step away from the everyday unconscious patterns that I tend to live my life mired in. A place where I can actually feel love and compassion from my sisters. I am reminded that I can live life in a different pattern. I can go into the world living from the love and compassion that is my heart.

Rita Vincent: It is a place where Jesus can be sitting on the floor leaning on our legs while we are in prayer. He is the "sacred center."

Jane DeBlieux: Sacred center is the manifestation of feminine energy . . . divine in nature . . . an energy that allows us to love one another along the journey that we ultimately take alone. This holy ground provides a safe haven for the exposure of pain, insecurities, and struggles, as well as our courage and successes. I feel the unseen presence of the grandmothers who came before us, watching, guiding, and smiling.

Elsa Mendoza: Where I am able to reconnect with the divine feminine—the soulful feminine—the wisdom soaked feminine, laughter borne out of deep reflection and healing. Where I can speak and feel understood not just listened to. It's a gathering where *I experience encounter not merely meeting up. It's a thread of friendship beyond words and where spoken words are not always necessary: Sacred Presence.*

Velma Cheramie: I started going to Sacred Center at my friend Avis's invitation. We were a handful of women seeking a way to grow in our faith. The practice of being in contemplation together is so fulfilling. The silence, singing birds, acorns dropping on the roof, gentle rain— these gifts are the tangible presence of God as we are embraced in His love and experience authentic transformation deep within our souls.

Wendi Romero: Sacred Center is a "holding place" for me, where the joys and sorrows of life are acknowledged, affirmed, and held with love.

And so the meditations you will read in this book come out of these experiences of Sacred Center. They are written by women just like you. Each writing comes from the heart, and we hope that they speak to women's experiences: our hurts and joys, our struggles and our bliss. Thomas Merton writes, "To live selfishly is to bear life as an intolerable burden; when we are selfless, we live in joy, realizing that the experience of life itself is love and gift."

We humbly seek to share our experiences of life and of God. These meditations are an invitation to spend some days wrapped in shared wisdom, protected by the strength and joy that is the Spirit as she dances upon the earth.

How to use this book:

Dear Readers,

We have divided the book into sections that are designed to be used for each week of your prayer. You will need a companion journal to write down your thoughts and feelings about the daily readings. This book is a bit different, in that it is designed to be written in as well! You can use the last two days of the week to record on the blank pages of the book anything that has stirred during the week.

At Sacred Center, we value the inner promptings that each person experiences. We have been told and told what to think, feel, and believe. We think it is time to find the wisdom within, the unique murmurings of the self and the dance with Spirit within.

Enjoy the offering of this book that comes from so many. Take your time. You may want to paint mandalas, make your own poetry, or listen to music as you go. Go deeply, go quietly, go with love.

—Lyn Holley Doucet

Do What You Must

If space to breathe
is what you need,
make room for it.

If the quiet is calling,
remove yourself from
all that disturbs you.

If peace is what you prefer,
don't contribute to
the chaos of the world.

If stillness is what you seek,
slow down the frantic pace
at which you move.

If courage is summoned,
dig into your own ground
and pull it to the surface.

If love underlies all that you do,
it must first be found in you,
then sent out to others too.

In the window of this vast universe
you're wildly passing through,
simply do what you must do.

—Wendi Romero

Noticing God

Photo by Rita Vincent

Day 1

It Was You

I sat in quiet this morning
trying to release my thoughts.

As the silence crept around me
I began to feel a strange sensation.

It felt like a warm stream entering my body,
it was golden in appearance,
and it began to filter
through my whole body.

I let it happen,
it was an odd feeling but good also.
And I know it was You
holding me, loving me, and healing me!

Thank you

—Michelle deLaunay

For your day: *I can live only a moment at a time. So much can be
realized in a single moment.*

Day 2

Mine is the sunlight, mine is the morning, born of the One Light. Praise every morning, God's re-creation of a new day. —Traditional

Morning Has Broken

I'm pondering my favorite part of the day, the morning. The Cat Stevens's popular version of the song "Morning Has Broken" has always touched me. At my first retreat in 1998, I made a promise to myself and to my Lord that I would rise earlier, just to spend time with Him. With my age and all that goes with it—hormones decreasing, night sweats, interrupted sleep—I have no trouble waking earlier to be in His presence. There is calm in the morning that I desperately need to start each day in a chaotic world.

I make a cup of coffee; grab my Bible, other books and my journal, as soon as I open my eyes. My journaling daily has become another avenue of prayer. Letters to my Heavenly Father, sharing with Him daily activities, sharing my joys, sharing my sadness and constantly letting Him know how grateful I am for all of it has become my favorite part of the day. For me, it's all about praying, waiting, trusting, hoping and, above all, loving.

While I read, I make notes in the margins, marking a star at a sentence or a word that feeds me. I underline statements, quotes, scripture. I can feel God speaking to me. He constantly shows me the exact words I need for that very day. What an amazing blessing.

By doing these things every morning, I am gathering strength, peace, and direction for the day. Perhaps one day when I am no longer here, my children and grandchildren can read my writings, see my markings, and know how much I loved them and my Lord. Even after I'm gone, I can still be an example of God's grace, mercy, compassion, and love.

Morning has broken, and I see the beauty in sunrises, and I listen to the doves cooing, while watching the birds fly, and noticing the dew on every blade of grass. When I am present to the moment, mornings are the best part of my day.

—Denise Broussard

For your day: *Think about your favorite time of day. How can you be present to each day and sense God's presence?*

Day 3

If we open our eyes and our hearts, we see God's presence everywhere and in everything. His reveal is divine in our daily lives, giving us constant reminders that He is here with us.

God's Reveal

I see Him.
I see Him in the natural beauty that surrounds us.
He is the trust of the setting sun and the faith that a new day will come.
He is the hope of springtime and the patience of blossoms.
He is the kindness of a breeze and the grace of an eagle's flight.
He is the peace of the nighttime forest and presence of a mountain range.
I see Him.
I see Him in the miracle of birth.
He is the innocence of a newborn, the devotion of parenthood, and the desire to know happiness.
He is the strength in suffering, the compassion of serving others, and the forgiveness of injustice.
He is life in death and the face of our soul.
He is love.
I see Him.
I see Him in you.

—Jill Duhon

For your day: *Where do you see God?*

Day 4

Presence to the present. . . . is like the concentrated wonder of a parent holding a newborn.
—David Hass, Coming Home to Your True Self, 86

Present to the Presence

Being present to the Presence asks us to stop, be still, and embrace the silence.

To take yourself into a quiet room and sit quietly in a chair for a while is certainly countercultural. The first few times you do this, the ego might make you very uncomfortable, demanding that you get up and *do something!*

As we sit quietly in contemplative or centering prayer, we might breathe in a word or phrase that helps us stay focused, such as *love, Jesus, peace,* or *let go.*

Our minds continue chattering away as we settle in, hearts open to God. We open, we breathe, we stay, we wait. We watch as did the virgins with their lamps, waiting on the Bridegroom.

As I type this reflection, I look out at my patio and observe a statue of Jesus, the Sacred Heart. How many days and nights did Jesus wait during his life, up in the purple hills or in the sandy dust of the desert? How often did he hear answers—and how often did he leave his prayer with more questions? How long did it take before his Sacred Heart blazed forth in *all* its beauty?

And yet we can trust that, as we sit quietly in prayer, the Spirit does the work, stripping away the unnecessary and false and lighting our hearts with love. Have the courage today to take some time to sit quietly. Breathe in God's love. Maybe you will be led into wonder.

—Lyn Holley Doucet

For your day: *I will be present to the Presence.*

Day 5

And that is where God is-in the complicated things.
—Gary, in Jan L. Richardson's In the Sanctuary of Women, 242

In the Complicated Things

In the places of ecstatic joy or deep despair
—there is God
In the places where I am tongue-tied by grief and cannot put two words
together
—there is God
In the places where I feel too deeply as I look into my lover's eyes and
laughter bursts forth
—there is God
In the places where I am overwhelmed by anger and the poison it releases in me
—there is God
In the places where I have no words or too many words
—there is God
In the places where I am confronted with situations in which there are no
good solutions
—there is God
In the places where I am surrounded by indescribable beauty, beyond words
or pictures
—there is God
In the places where I don't understand myself
—there is God
In all those places,
the places of hurt,
the places of joy,
the places of hate,
the places of love,
in the simple things,
in the complicated things
—there is God

—Trudy Gomez

For your day: *Be gentle and merciful with yourself today, for in the center*
of it all, there is God.

Day 6

Noticing God: Notes from My Life

Day 7

Lovely Rituals

Day 8

Now it came to pass in those days that Jesus went out to the mountain to pray and continued all night in prayer to God.
—Luke 6:12

Where is your Mountain?

It's funny that I'm thinking about, *where is my mountain?* It can be a retreat center or my back yard, or it can be my bed. My bed, in my room, is exactly where I step out of the busyness of life to sit and pray daily, most days.

Matthew 6:6: "But when you pray, go into your room, close the door and pray to your Father, who is unseen. Then your Father who sees what is done in secret will reward you." Reward? I think of peace, hope, love, and His forgiveness.

Whether I begin at 4:43 a.m., as I did this morning, or 5:30 or 7:00, I sit still in silence for up to an hour, seven days a week, just to be in His presence. I gather strength, courage, wisdom, and love, to make it, just for today. I hold so many others in love, cherishing the individual nature of each. I hold so many in their pain, suffering, addictions, deaths, illnesses, etc. Yes, we are all so different, but all are one, so connected.

I also read; and I journal, which I have turned into love and venting letters to my Lord. I have learned to go to Him for everything. His journey was a constant life of crisis, and so is ours, at times. This is the reason I need to go with Him to the mountain to pray, go off to a solitary place, led by the Spirit into the wilderness, a deserted place. My journey has been an uphill climb of trials and all sorts of temptations. An easy life would have meant missing life's deepest meanings. My strong faith with total dependence on God came only from facing abandonment, sexual abuse, addictions, and frustration. I would not change a thing even if I could. Yes, I ponder all these things on a sacred mountain, the one I find in my very own bed.

Then other mountain times can take place at a retreat center. I don't have to go far to get what I need, but I just need to go. Once a year met my needs in the past, but now I seek more and more silence because it is where I have received the most healing and peace. There I can relax, knowing and trusting that God is with me and with my family while I'm gone. Anytime I say yes to spending time with Him and His creation, it is amazing. I've learned so many things in my silence; this is a way I care for myself. We must take care of ourselves first, if we are ever to help anyone else. Yes, I went through some trauma as a young child and as an adult, but I know now, through silence, there was a part of me untouched, unharmed, and not hurt, and that place of Love is what pulled me out of the darkness into His light.

—Denise Broussard

For your day: *Where is your mountain or deserted place in which you can take care of yourself?*

Day 9

Then let us drink a cup of tea. Silence descends.
—Muriel Barbery

The Philosophy of Tea

For the past twenty-five years or so, I have found that having a cup of tea is a much favored way to allow myself a break in my day. Sometimes Jerry and I meet around the tea kettle at about three in the afternoon to prepare a cup of tea and have a small nibble of something. This is as much to sit and slow down as it is to satisfy the needed boost between lunch and dinner. We have a large selection of tea, but he usually goes for the black tea and I skip around, usually landing on an herbal blend.

Coffee was the hot drink of choice for my family when I was growing up and when I was raising my children. We also drank lots of very sweet iced tea. I never got to know the joy of a cup of tea until I met Jerry.

Jerry and I are both enchanted with the idea of tea ceremony, and we enjoy the thought of a real ceremony as we pour, steep, flavor, and savor our own cup of tea—even choosing just the right cup. One day we will visit a city where we can find an authentic Japanese Tea Ceremony served by a tea master; this is definitely on our list.

The reason I speak of tea here is because, for me, there is serenity around making the tea. As I go about the process of preparing the tea things and making the tea, I usually come to a quiet within. I don't hurry tea making as I am apt to hurry other tasks. I don't really know why, but I seem to be more present in the preparation of tea.

I want to take that presence and quiet to my other tasks. I am told that when we are peaceful and mindful in the preparation of our food, the food is more digestible and nourishing. I am certain that if I were to go about my routines with the peace of the tea making, then my home would be more peaceful. I want this philosophy of tea to extend to all that I do, all those I encounter, and everything I touch. We know and are very aware that we can never obtain peace in our world until we make peace within.

—Avis Lyons LeBlanc

For your day: *Which of your tasks call you to be present?*

Day 10

And the smoke of incense, with the prayers of the saints, went up before God out of the angel's hand.
—Revelation 8:4

Morning Prayer

It is still dark out.

The time just before dawn, when the moon is making its

final descent to give way to a new day.

I begin my morning ritual.

A bicycle ride as my dog lopes by my side.

I smell cigar smoke wafting through the cool morning mist

before I can see its origin.

As I round the corner,

I see the red tip embers of rolled tobacco

clinched in the front teeth of an elderly man.

We pass each other and bow our heads.

Not a word is spoken.

The man's feet planted firmly on the earth,

mine on the pedals of a bike,

as our four-legged friends run freely beside us.

We are up before light, being touched by Great Mystery.

Our morning prayers are lifted like incense

on the smoke from his Cuban cigar.

— Patty Prather

For your day: *Today, stay attuned to God's presence in prayer and in the ordinary events of a normal day.*

16

Day 11

Reflection after Adoration of the Holy Eucharist

I often pray the Rosary when I go to Adoration every Monday morning and I meditate on the Joyful Mysteries. In the first decade, the mystery of The Annunciation, St. Gabriel declares to Mary:

"Hail favored one! The Lord is with you. Do not be afraid Mary, for you have found favor with God. Behold, you will conceive in your womb and bear a son and you shall name him Jesus. He will be great and will be called Son of the Most High and the Lord God will give him the throne of David his father and he will rule over the house of Jacob forever and of his kingdom there will be no end."
—**Luke 1:28-33**

Mary said "Yes."
As I pray this decade, I think on the power behind Mary's yes. Her yes changed all of human history. Her yes was so outside the normal realm of the world she lived in.
Have you ever read scripture and inserted yourself as one of the characters in the story and tried to imagine what you would have done in that situation? I put myself in Mary's shoes, and I wonder how I would have reacted to such a calling. I hear myself saying to St. Gabriel, "Do you know how the people in my community would think of me and treat me? Who will believe that I was impregnated by the Holy Spirit? Joseph will never marry me if this happens!"
Oh ye, of such little faith am I. I am so grateful that St. Gabriel was sent to the Blessed Virgin Mary and not to me. Because of her 'yes', all humanity was given a chance for salvation through the birth of her son, Jesus Christ. She willingly said yes, in spite of her fears, and moved forward in what God asked of her.
Mary trusted in God.

"And behold, Elizabeth, your relative, has also conceived a son in her old age, and this is the sixth month for her who was called barren; for nothing will be impossible for God."
—*Luke 1:36-37*

While praying the second decade, the mystery of the Visitation, I look at how the Blessed Virgin Mary runs to her cousin, Elizabeth, immediately upon learning from St. Gabriel that she too has been blessed by God. Elizabeth, in her very old age, is in the sixth month of her pregnancy. When Elizabeth hears Mary's greeting, her infant leaps in her womb, and Mary proclaims her Magnificat:

"My soul proclaims the greatness of the Lord; my spirit rejoices in God Savior. For he has looked upon his handmaid's lowliness; behold, from now on will all ages call me blessed. The Mighty One has done great things for me, and holy is his name. His mercy is from age to age to those who fear him."
—*Luke 1:46-50*

Mary served and supported Elizabeth. She rejoiced in God's blessings and was filled with gratitude.

While praying and meditating on these two decades, my mind gently turned toward thoughts of my Sacred Center sisters. Every Thursday morning, we gather, eager to see one another and visit, listen to, and pray for one anothers needs. Together we are joyful, sorrowful, loving, and accepting of one another.

Mary found "favor with God" and "all ages call her blessed." God blesses us individually with grace-filled moments. Together we celebrate those moments by our yes in speaking of our joys and sorrows; we trust in God that he hears our prayers, and we are filled with gratitude for His presence.

As I pray, I hear the Spirit speaking to my soul in a soft whisper: *This is our own 'little' way; our little magnificat.*

Every time we gather, we are saying 'yes' to God and 'yes' to each sister. We come together to stand by one another in our weaknesses, to grow in faith, and to overcome those shortcomings. We pray for one another, and we pray for our world. Together, we rejoice over the multitude of graces God bestows upon us at our every gathering and throughout our lives.

I am so grateful to be one of our Sacred Center sisters. We do say 'yes', we trust in God in our frailties, and we pray for one another following the example of the Blessed Virgin Mary.

Lord Jesus Christ, may you continue to bless us with your graces, expand our hearts and minds to serve you, first in our humanity and in your beautiful creation. Amen.

—Velma LeBlanc Cheramie

For your day: *Watch for the grace-filled moments in your day; receive, pray, and trust that God is with you in your every thought and walks beside you in your every step. Just say "Yes".*

Day 12

Until you've found the fire inside yourself, you won't reach the spring of life.
—Rumi

In the Cave of My Heart

As I enter this space of quiet, I leave behind the chatter of the head, thinking to listen to the heart. I arrive to the rhythmic drumbeat of my heart, welcoming me to this space where spirit thrives. I walk around in wonder, noticing the flame of God's love—the warmth of it inviting me to sit and rest awhile with the Presence of all that is.

I gaze into the flame blazing within me and see my reflection. It looks different because within me is the glow of God's love surrounding me. The voice says, "Let go, release all that holds you from hearing my voice and receiving my love." With the energy and enthusiasm of His presence, I get up, reaching for His extended hand, and we dance around the fire to the drumbeat of my heart. We are one. The voice says, "Dance this oneness with others you meet on your spirit's journey. This is your gift of abundant love to be shared with others."

—Pat Low

For your day: *What is Spirit calling you to share with others today?*

Day 13

Lovely Rituals: Notes from My Life

Day 14

Graces of Creation

Photo by Wendi Romero

Day 15

The trees grow in silence. . . . Silence gives us a new perspective.
—Mother Teresa

The Gift of Nature

I lie under the magnificent oak trees, with the sun peeking in and out of the branches, warming my heart, inviting me to feel God's presence. The gentle breeze, which is uncharacteristic for a hot August day, flows over me like a security blanket. I listen to the music of the crickets and cicadas. Sometimes the sounds rise to such heights, as if applauding God's joy. Other times they descend to a whisper, allowing the refrain of the breeze to harmonize in the creation of nature. The moss hangs gently within the branches and leaves, a wisdom symbol of just being, not clinging.

While taking in the sights and sounds around me, I noticed a dragonfly perched on top of a twig. It remained there in the stillness for several minutes. The dragonfly seemed to know the importance of stillness to hear the gentle voice of God.

In contrast, a butterfly flitted in the grass, never able to find the right place to land. The life of the butterfly was trying to take in everything and not stopping long enough to enjoy anything. The contrast of the two reminded me of Martha and Mary. Martha was busy about many things, while Mary sat at the feet of Jesus to listen to His message.

When am I a Martha when God is calling me to be Mary? Nature brings me to a Mary moment. My heart is filled with gratitude.

—Pat Low

For your Day: *Sit quietly in nature. What do you hear or see in the silence?*

Day 16

In the Celtic tradition, it is said that in creation there are places that are translucent and God's glory shines through. I believe there are places and experiences where this is true; these are called Thin Places.

Thin Places

In thin places we meet
the veil so transparent
the division of the mundane and the divine
so close, so separate
Sitting on the beach when dawn breaks
Mist touching my cheek on a foggy morning
Lying in the grass, clouds floating by
Light and shadows playing on canyon walls
Real Presence: wind playing in my hair
Breath of a child on my neck
Rustle of dry leaves
Recording memories in mind, body, and spirit
Logic is put aside
No barriers exist
Laws of time and space suspend
Communing with God
Feeling God
Experiencing the mystery
A Presence greater than myself
Surrendering to the Holy

—Trudy Gomez

For your day: *How will you open yourself to experience God today?*

Day 17

When Lyn told me the title of her book of meditations on the life of Hildegard of Bingen, <u>Light on a River's Turning</u>, I was fascinated by the feeling the words evoked in me. It was as if I was about to see around a turning of my own, and I knew it was beautiful.

Walking by the River

The single-circuit labyrinth of flat slabs of slate, stained rust and brown and beige from their life within the earth, are beautifully laid out near to the edge of the Vermilion River. Drawn as I was to stand near the river, I was drawn also to the offering of the simple walking meditation.

I walked the labyrinth barefoot, which is very natural to me, allowing me to feel more connected to the earth and grounded in this place. Even as I walked, looking at the next stone, and the next, I was aware of the water so near me because of the cool wetness of the air and the smell—musty and muddy—as the river moved past. This winding brown ribbon of the Vermilion River that I love so much, and the circuitous stones placed alongside it, created a feeling of joy and abundance within me. I often go in memory to this peaceful and easy time to bring it to myself again and again.

I stopped in places on the labyrinth that face the river's turn north or faced the bend to the south. I breathed in the wetness of the close-by water. I watched the current pull and push branches and debris along its path. I watched the glint of sun on the ripples as I stood on a cool, rust-colored stone. I moved on and was stopped by the deep shadows of the trees on the water on the far side of the river.

The river moves on as I watch, unaware even of my watching, of my little life. This great river has great things to do. I imagine the places it is moving toward, and the saying comes to me, *you never step in the same river twice.* I recognize that I will never step into the same moment of my life again, and I wonder if I want to hold on or if I want to let go. So much in a life to contemplate, and I am grateful for this life that allows me to do so.

—Avis Lyons LeBlanc

For your day*: Breathe into one of your own treasured experiences and feel the gift again. Maybe you will find a new gift.*

Day 18

Then God said: Let earth bring forth vegetation: every kind of plant that bears seed and every kind of fruit tree on earth that bears fruit with its seed in it....God said: Let the earth bring forth every kind of living creature: tame animals, crawling things, and every kind of wild animal. And so it happened...God saw that it was good.

Genesis 1:11

Earth Day

Let us give thanks for all the animals that roam the earth, and for all the seed bearing plants that live so that humans may have life. The sky and the seas, the mountains and the rivers, all of creation was set into motion before the birth of man.

I am humbled by the realization that man cannot survive a week without the plants and animals for nourishment, but plants and animals do not need man for their survival. They would go on living if man never existed.

When I ponder that all on earth would keep evolving without man's presence I am brought to my knees in humility, gratitude and awe, giving thanks to God for all the living creatures who sacrifice their lives in order that humans may live on this planet.

May we all awaken to becoming good stewards of this planet we call home. Amen.

—Patty Prather

For your day: *List the ways you can be a better steward of God's creation.*

Day 19

I love God's shadow better than man's light.
— Madame Swetchine

In the Shadow of Giants

A slight breeze blows through the grove.

Sunlight warming my back.

Soft paths of moss cushioning my step.

My shadow hidden in the shadow of the sequoia's giant shadow.

My being swallowed into the the giant sequoia's spirit.

The Giant tree is 267 feet taller than me.

It is as tall as a 25 story building.

Its circumference is 68 feet greater than mine.

This living tree has lived for 2,937 years longer than I.

This tree began breathing air almost 1,000 years before Jesus' birth!

The human body contains 13 gallons of water.

The Giant tree before me can drink 500 to 800 gallons of water a day.

It will produce 60 million seeds in its lifetime.

A woman will produce 400,000 eggs.

Of these eggs only 20 mature each month and only one is released.

Out of the Sequoia's 60 million seeds, only three or four will grow to be a hundred years old.

Great Mystery whispers to me, "You had 3 seeds, and they have had six seeds that might live the next 90 years.

I hear your wish for them. The wish that at least once in their lifetime they also can stand in the shadow of a Giant Sequoia and know their Creator."

I hear Great Mystery whispering on the wind in the grove.

"My beloved, I have walked with you today, as you have become lost in the Giants of my creation."

I have given you this gift today.

Spend your winter years pondering the magnificence of all of my creation."

—Patty Prather

For your day: *What places in nature does God call you hear his voice through his creation? Describe how you feel when you think of this place?*

Day 20

Graces of Creation: Notes from My Life

Day 21

Silence and Center

Day 22

Life is often lived at a frantic pace, so much so that it becomes normal to us. It's hard to drink deeply of Spirit when we are frantic and harried. Take some time today to calm down and relax deeply.

Calming Down

I think that I could pray, if I could just calm down.
If I could quiet my mind and stop living in
the future with anxiety,
the past with regret.
I have heard it said, many times, that the only reality is
Now. I breathe this in, I believe it.
I completely relax my body; I stop holding on to my list of things to do.
Right now: I sit in this chair.
Right now: I am breathing in, I am breathing out.
Right now: I am opening to a quiet space where God lives in bright darkness,
offering himself to me with each breath.
Christ anoints me, Christ holds me, Christ breathes in me.
I am calm and open. I Belong.

—Lyn Holley Doucet

For your day: *May I be calm.*

Day 23

As we put our endless mind chatter aside, we can enter the grace of the present moment. We can hear the true voice of love. Calm down, let go, and find that sacred place within.

Centering

Listen to the Spirit
speaking to you in the silence of your Heart,
yearning for the call,
surrendering self to what is—the present.
Stay in this place where your soul is nourished,
filled with the Grace of the present moment.
Put words aside so that you can listen
to the true words of love.
That is grace.
That is God.

—Pat Low

For your day: *You are centered in the Spirit of Love.*

Day 24

Sometimes it is the most wounded experiences that draw forth the greatest growth and movement of the Spirit within us. After you read this experience, you might want to journal about where grace has come through suffering in your own life.

The Gift in Silence

Our God is amazing. "Amazing grace, how sweet the sound that saved a wretch like me. I once was lost, but now am found. 'Twas blind but now I see." This song always comes to mind when I look back at where I was and how far I've come, my Lord with me the whole time. He has brought me through a challenging journey, with brokenness that began in my mother's womb. I wasn't even aware of a feeling of abandonment caused by my father until I was praying and God revealed it to me. And He revealed that through the brokenness and suffering, He led me to wholeness and strength, and that I would never feel alone again.

A great shift happened during this time of silence. Instead of labeling my experiences as bad—sexual abuse, abandonment, the deaths of so many I loved, and all the battles with addiction—I realized two things: First of all, I am healed through Christ of my negative experiences. Second, and most important, I now see evidence that I was being prepared as a mother through the things I endured. I prayed that my children would never have to go through the trials I experienced. My prayers were answered in a different way; my children's trials began even earlier in life than mine did.

I had been prepared to be compassionate and supportive, loving them unconditionally, as our Father is compassionate with us. And somehow I know that they, too, are being prepared as well. Their hearts have been broken open, like mine, to hold love and to be compassionate. Yes, God is amazing.

—Denise Broussard

For your day: *Sometimes it is the most wounded experiences that draw forth the greatest growth and movement of the Spirit within us when we are still and sit in silence.*

Day 25

Be still and confess that I am God! I am exalted among the nations, exalted on the earth. The Lord of hosts is with us; our stronghold is the God of Jacob.
—Psalm 46:11–12

When Our World Is Quiet

When our world is quiet, our breathing slows
and the soft beat of our hearts can be heard.
Landscapes come alive.
The tongue and throat rest
while the mind's eye springs open.
The veil thins,
a shimmering,
a silent message from a still, small voice.
Consciousness expands.
Mystery abounds.
Spirit travels divine mists
collecting secrets whispered to the soul.
Reverberations of peace, hope and love,
calming the storm of life.
Allelluia! Emmanuel!

—Velma LeBlanc Cheramie

For your day: *Allow yourself to experience the deep peace that God gives. Go to your "alone" place. Breathe in peace deeply, breathing out all your worries, sending them to God who is our stronghold. Breathe in his undying love, his mercy, his peace, his Presence.*

Day 26

Centering prayer has become an important part of my life. There is so much I'm unaware of unless I take time to be still, breathe deeply, and place my awareness on what lies at the heart of me.

If Not For

If not for the center,
there wouldn't be two
sides to anything.

If not for the valley,
there wouldn't be
twin peaks.

If not for the running river,
there wouldn't be
outer banks.

If not for the present,
there wouldn't be
a future or a past.

We sit in circles
pondering
this great mystery

equidistant to the edges
of everything.
Only the center truly knows.

—Wendi Romero

For your day: *May I become aware of the power of centeredness*

Day 27

Silence and Center: Notes from My Life

Day 28

Family Stories

Photo by Rita Vincent

Day 29

Faith of Our Fathers

On May 23, 2015, we attended the baptism
and naming ceremony for our grandson,
Soren Vincent Hofherr.
This was a Catholic/Jewish ceremony
performed at the home of our daughter
and son-in-law in Maryland.
The priest and rabbi are good friends
and rode to the house together.
(I wish the rest of the world acted this way.)
Soren was given the Hebrew name
Rafi after his paternal grandmother, Rose,
meaning noble, and Katriel for
Vincent, meaning victor.
He was welcomed into two faiths and
two families, along with their traditions.
He was oblivious to the family dynamics going on.
He only knew he was loved
and that he was being touched by the Holy Spirit.
Afterward, "someone" gave Soren to his Pops to hold.
Soren opened his mouth and leaned in to give
Pops three big open-mouth kisses.
Soren Vincent Hofherr, Rafi Katriel, noble victor,
breathed in the faith of his fathers.
Kissed by an angel.
Kissed by the spirit of God!

—Rita B. Vincent

For your day: *Do I see God in faiths other than my own? When did I feel kissed by the spirit of God?*

Day 30

Whole people see and create wholeness wherever they go; split people see and create splits in everything and everybody.
—Fr. Richard Rohr

Lessons in Live and Let Live

I get to laugh at myself almost daily because of the blessing of having my twenty-seven-year-old granddaughter in my life regularly. Not only is she lots of fun and we get to laugh a lot, but she also shows me, consistently, where many of my prejudices and judgments of others are alive and well and kicking up control issues. She hasn't cured me yet, but I don't usually tell her my little secrets. I do see them clearer, and I truly do want to mend my splits.

She has a very open, trusting, and happy worldview. She does have her own judgments, they just seem so few and so compassionate compared to mine. If I comment about someone in a negative way she might say, *Maybe she doesn't have a Grandma to help her.* Or, *I don't see that,* said so sweetly. She truly believes most of us are just doing the best we can. I think that is true; I just don't always remember it.

When she came to live in Lafayette last June, I was concerned about people seeing her tattoos that run from her fingertips all the way up her arms. I still don't understand the need for tattoos, but I am accepting her with hers. Hello Kitty and LOVE and such. I find that I no longer notice the tattoos and I am surprised when others do. Progress, you might say. Not so much. I still don't get it, and she can't explain it except that she loves them. But I do get her. I do find myself less judgmental of the tattoos on other young people I see. They are all finding their way just as I have to find mine; we just do it differently.

She chooses her friends based on how good and kind they are. She sees color, gender, age, and appearance but doesn't see those things as a factor. Kind is high on her list of desirable friends and how they treat her and others. Clean and fairly well spoken seem to be of some importance. I haven't been able to pinpoint criteria, but she isn't particular as to affluent or poor, where they live, what they do for a living as long as they want a good life and are willingly going that direction. I would have picked through all that and choose those who are most like me. I am stretching in that respect because of how close she is and how her daily life is connected to mine.

I have to remind myself over and over again what is my business and what is not my business. It's constant, and it means that sometimes I have to swallow my words or bite my tongue. I remind myself that her life is not mine, her journey is not mine, and it is not my business except to the extent that I love her. She will make her way just as I did. She chooses what is now and where she is going.

I am fortunate that she enjoys my company, she seeks me out as a companion, and she is very open about her life. I sometimes give her advice, but I couch it in offering her choices and then say, *Do what feels right for you.* I sometimes even mean it when I say it, and sometimes I am hoping she takes my advice.

I am learning about true inclusion. I am learning about acceptance of others' viewpoints and how they don't have to do life as I do to make them ok. And, usually, they are really nice and good people. I just wish I was learning more quickly and taking it in more deeply.

She is learning a broader perspective in life also. She is learning that she has choices she didn't realize before now and that she might need to give a little more consideration to the next step. I think we make a pretty good team. We help each other. I am grateful for her in my life.

—Avis Lyons LeBlanc

For your day: *Is there a position you take that makes others wrong and yourself right? How might that be keeping you from rejoicing with others?*

Day 31

And He departed from our sight that we might return to our heart, and there find Him. For He departed, and behold, He is here. —St Augustine

Resurrection after My Father's Death

I relive his excruciating pain, as his muscles twitched from the touch of my too-cold hand upon his arm.
What more could I have done to ease his pain? Soft music, soft light from candles, massages with emu-oil could not alleviate the excruciating pain.

Time seemed to be traveling faster than the speed of light; his mind was gone, his spirit departed. I had failed him.
His heart was still beating, his hand clutching a stranger's finger as if clinging desperately for life.

His silent scream that only I could hear, deafening my soul.
"DON'T LEAVE ME. I WANT TO HOLD ON. I AM AFRAID OF LEAVING."

I could not stop the virulent enemy from its swift battle within him. It swept through his bloodstream as quickly and powerfully as a brush fire that started from a random bolt of lightning. I desperately searched for balance.

I was pulled by the needs of others.
I cannot be all things to everyone.
I am a mere mortal wanting to be still in my grief.
I beg to be given the gift of being alone with my grief.
I will renew.
I will be reborn.

Jesus stayed three days in the tomb before He rose.
It has been just three days since I laid my life's teacher in the cold, rain-soaked earth.

I want to stay in the tomb a little longer, before my resurrection.

—Patty Prather

For your day: *When have you needed to just be alone in your grief? What spiritual tools aided you in experiencing a resurrection after such an experience?*

Day 32

The Cold

On this day, a day like the others,
my stomach has a familiar ache
like a knife searing my insides.
Maybe I should have eaten,
but that isn't it.

As strange faces rush past
I look at Mama and there it is
her smile, so gentle, so loving
how could she possibly smile
sitting in this place, waiting
waiting to be wheeled away,
wondering what news she will receive today?
Will this be a good day?
What *is* a good day when you are dying?

And then he appears
the orderly, stone-faced
with the wheelchair.
Why can't he at least smile?
Why can't he be nice to her for just one moment?
Doesn't he have a mother?
I want to shake him
for God's sake, be nice to my Mama.

She is so frail,
trembling as she slides her tiny body into the seat
and off they go.
She says such nice things to him.
He answers but I can tell he doesn't care.
And then there is silence.
She's just another patient.

I try my best to keep up
but again, no conversation,
no empathy on his part,
not even a gentle ride.
This time it is a rough one,
her little hands gripping the armrests.
Can't he tell she is hurting and needs gentle care?

Finally, reaching radiology,
he parks her and says *here we are.*
He briskly walks away.
Yes, here we are.
Thanks for all your *compassion.*

It's *cold.*
There's no one or no thing in the hall but a stretcher.
I cover her with a blanket.
She is cold.
She stays cold.
Why does everything have to be so cold?

I know
and she knows.
Sometimes it's scary knowing things.

—Jane DeBlieux

For your day*: Today, search for a way to be gentle and compassionate toward others.*

Day 33

I praise you because I am fearfully and wonderfully made; your
works are wonderful, I know that full well.
—Psalm 139:14

Happy Birthday, Mom

My mother missed her 87th birthday by two months; she died on February 5, 2017. Neither Mom nor her daughters thought she would be with us as long as she was.

There would be no writings from me if it weren't for my mom. She did bring me into this world, and I thanked her for that all the time.

I first think of how much she loved us. Her two daughters came first. She nurtured us in the only way she knew how. We were never without good meals, clothes, a clean home (as in, we-took-off-our-shoes-at-the-door clean). She did all she could to make our lives comfortable.

She made sure we attended church every Sunday morning, Sunday night, and Wednesday night. Because of her insistence, I had a strong base to rely on later in life when trauma and tragedy hit. I do thank her for that because it saved my life many times.

Mom couldn't do many of the things she used to, and she had a hard time accepting that and finding her life's purpose. But I remember that she had such a green thumb and a love for her yard and her home. Taking so much care to make sure everything looked nice and in order. Anything she planted grew. She had a love for birds and squirrels, feeding them and watching them. I also admired her love of horses and dogs. Her exterior seemed hard, but her heart was really tender. As I think about it now, I realize that she nurtured all the living things that came into her circle.

And, of course, consider her talent for music. She could play any instrument she picked up. She couldn't read a sheet of music but played by ear. It was another of her amazing gifts, but I don't think she ever realized that, no matter how many times we told her. (Oh gosh, this is sounding familiar, as I have felt the same way in my own life.) She had so much talent and so much to offer but always put herself down.

She wanted to give us a life that would be better than the one she had growing up. She managed to do that with her deep wounds and her broken heart, along with a past she just couldn't forget.

We all must accept the past as past, without denying it or discarding it. Reminisce about it, but don't live in it. Learn from it, but don't punish ourselves about it or continually regret it. Just don't get stuck there. I believe we must learn to forgive ourselves and others, asking for forgiveness that will soften our hearts, drain the bitterness, and dissolve any guilt.

Our past is neither an accident nor a mistake. We have been where we needed to be with the necessary people. If we can embrace our history, with its pain, its imperfections, even its tragedies, as well as its blessings, we can realize it as uniquely ours.

—Denise Broussard

For your day: *Philippians 3:13-14: Brothers and sisters I do not consider myself yet to have taken hold of it. But one thing I do; forgetting what is behind and straining toward what is ahead. I press on toward the goal to win the prize for which God has called me heavenward in Christ Jesus.*

Day 34

Family Stories: Notes from My Life

Day 35

On the Journey

Day 36

Sometimes I grow frustrated about things I don't understand, and other times I marvel at the mystery of life.

Mystery

I walk in a world I cannot see
and do not understand.
My mind cannot comprehend
what lies beyond the veil-
the mystery of a Word
taking on form, breathing
and walking among us.
I walk in a world I can see
and still do not understand.
My mind cannot comprehend
that the beauty of a rose
and the pain of its thorn
are both inconceivable love.

—Wendi Romero

For your day: *May I experience the mystery of inconceivable love today.*

Day 37

I wrote this after walking a labyrinth with a beautiful group of women. I felt as if we were being watched from another realm. Those who walked before us watched as we came together seeking and thirsting for ourselves and for God. They smiled because they know what we will one day know. I felt as if we were in many ways one with those who had trod before us, a shared community of the seen and the unseen.

This Path

We yearn for the straight way
for no forks or turns or decisions to make,
nothing to hinder
what is considered
progress.

Hearts,
lest they deny themselves,
blossom in the curves and the bumps
realizing that the circle of life beckons saying
come, run with me.
The pause at every turn,
the curves, the unknown that hides beyond the hill
the decision that awaits with each breath
left - right
stop - move
fast – slow
open - closed
and so it goes.

Decide for me
the head screams.
Decide for me
the heart whimpers.
Restless, we watch as others pass
lovingly, pensive, expressionless, sad, happy.

Traveling alone
our souls thirst
for the core,
the center
the One.

This One
this all-encompassing love and compassion
this I Am
requires movement
requires change
transformation at each threshold
and yet, lovingly,
waits and does not push.

This journey,
this circle of life
this mystery of light in the dark,
seen but not seen this side of heaven,
remains just that.

And so we seek,
just as the flower leans into the sun,
this great unknowing
this ache in our heart
this path
this one solitary road to self
and to Him.

—Jane DeBlieux

For your day: *What does your path look like today?*

Day 38

I desire for my journey to be guided by my allowing and questioning in a receptive way. Asking for guidance, asking for help, and allowing spirit to respond and to guide, will free me up to enjoy and play more. Freedom is found by letting Spirit lead.

Guided-ness

Winter,
I follow you within.
I hold the quiet spaces
where Spirit meets me
and puts my feet on the path
to the emerging spring.
I am a part of
the unfolding journey.
I dance into my days
knowing
I am in charge
only
of the attitude
with which I meet my days.
Freedom is found
by letting Spirit lead.
My spirit can then roam,
poke around,
experiment,
living a life of happy guided-ness.

—Avis Lyons LeBlanc

For your day: *Notice if and how you receive and respond to your guided-ness.*

Day 39

I often hesitate to heed a call from within, however the tug at my heart doesn't leave. It stays until I'm ready to cross the next threshold that awaits me.

The Only Way Was Through It

The call came one day out of the blue, a summons
back to a place I already knew. The invitation was

a return to wakeful dreaming, to navigate night
during the light of day. I then heard a voice say

"Close your eyes or keep them open wide. What do
you see, smell, and hear? What does it look like, how

does it feel in this holy temple housed in skin?"
I see a stream running through it, cutting the middle

in a forest of green. Standing at the edge, I know
I've arrived at another shore. I stare into the water

and see not only my reflection, but a crossing that's
not too deep. I lower a naked foot and a rush hastens

up my spine. I'm taken in and held by a top layer of
soft silty slime. Slow and sinking, ankle-deep, I place

one foot then the other, until I reach the farther side.
Wet, cold, and muddy, I emerge in a bright clearing.

Basking in brilliant rays of warm sunlight, I realized
there was no way around it. The only way was through.

—Wendi Romero

For your day: *May I cross a new threshold today.*

Day 40

When our inner child is not nurtured and nourished, our minds gradually close to new ideas . . . .and surprises of the Spirit.
—**Brennan Manning**

The Game of Illusions

It is my sixty-fourth journey around the sun.

I am a grandmother, an elder still caring for her elder, who is in her ninth decade.

Childhood and teen-year memories have become reframed.

I have become a revisionist story teller in my own autobiography.

It is the last third of my time on earth, yet the years from infancy to young adulthood silently brood in my psyche. They are like ghosts who have put up permanent residence.

The fight-or-flight modes, the adrenaline rushes, stomach churning, decisions to remain silent, emotions stuffed deep into the recesses of my heart.

When these childhood ghosts emerge from the depths, ready to do battle, they often present themselves in physical forms that escalate into anxiety and fear, stealing my peace.

I acknowledge their presence. They are warning signals that I need to make a choice not to return to childhood ways.

These protective modes aided my psychological survival when I was a vulnerable child, but I am an elder now. I no longer need to play these roles. I give thanks for how they helped me as a child, and I watch them vanish.

I held an illusion of what family meant and what was expected of one's role as a daughter and as a sister. I struggled for years when others did not live up to my understanding of what it meant to be family.

Until one day a wise old friend told me to fold up my board game, put away all the little pieces that represent the different players in my life's drama and go home, because, not only in the present moment but since childhood, no one else on my childhood family's board has ever played by my definition of what family means.

It was a painful awareness, yet so liberating.

I folded up the game and boxed it up.

I was set free of a lifetime of illusions and expectations and had found the true inner child whom God created.

—Patty Prather

For your day: *Look for illusions you may be continuing to live out. If they are detrimental to growing deeper spiritually, thank them and let them go.*

Day 41

On the Journey: Notes from My Life

Day 42

Pondering My Faith

Photo by Trudy Gomez

Day 43

Yes

Where did that "Yes" come from, the one that Mary said?
Where did that trust come from that led her to accept?
How did she have the courage to make the choice,
the one that looked foolish from an outsider's point of view?
How many wouldas, couldas, shouldas occur in my life?
How many messages and opportunities did I ignore?
Why do I choose to live in the "Caution Zone"?

—Trudy Gomez

For your day: *Do I dare pray, "Lord, give me the courage to say Yes
and then step into the abyss that is You"?*

Day 44

Ahab told Jezebel all that Elijah had done—that he had murdered all the prophets by the sword. Jezebel then sent a messenger to Elijah and said, "May the gods do thus to me and more, if by this time tomorrow I have not done with your life what was done to each of them." Elijah was afraid and fled for his life, ... he went a day's journey into the wilderness, until he came to a solitary broom tree and sat beneath it. He prayed for death: "Enough, LORD! Take my life, for I am no better than my ancestors." He lay down and fell asleep ... but suddenly a messenger* touched him and said, "Get up and eat!" He looked and there at his head was a hearth cake and a jug of water. After he ate and drank, he lay down again, but the angel of the LORD came back a second time, touched him, and said, "Get up and eat or the journey will be too much for you!" He got up, ate, and drank; then strengthened by that food, he walked forty days and forty nights to the mountain of God, Horeb.
—1 Kings 19:4-8

Elijah had just experienced a mountaintop miracle, and you would think that he wouldn't have been afraid of Jezebel's threats. He had just called on the power of God, and then he was down in the dumps and mumbling and complaining. He had seen the power of God. God had answered his prayer. He had been so confident then, and now he was so despondent that he forgot the saving power of God.

I can be the same way. I know God works in my life and that prayers are answered. But then something happens, and I seem to develop a case of temporary amnesia. I'm not so sure it is losing faith as much as it is losing energy, but I don't do what it takes to recharge. I don't partake of the things that will feed me: prayer, sacraments, gratitude.

God continually whispers in my ear, "Okay I love you! I want to be part of you. Here is my body, take and eat. I want to be such a part of you that you can't tell where I leave off and you begin. I want to nourish you. I am your food for the journey. Draw on me. I am your daily bread."

—Trudy Gomez

For your day: How will you let God nourish you today?

Day 45

Heart Recognizes Home

I can sit in the belly of darkness
Hostage of
... fear
... anger
... guilt
... helplessness
... not enoughness
I can sit in the belly of darkness
Acid eating away at my being.
Then a moment speaks
... a word
... an image
... a smell
... a sound
... a person
A moment speaks, "Ah-ha"
It lights a spark.
A spark that holds hopes and dreams when all had seemed lost,
Spark lights spark
Starting a fire that burns bright
Warming that cold space,
That desolate place
The place that was asleep,
Bring forth more and more light.
Light that inspires,
Where truth is illuminated.
Beauty comes forth.
Treasure is revealed.
Chasing away fear,
Overcoming anger,
Obliterating guilt,
No longer helpless,
Empowered.
Love shows itself in a moment
Like that little flash of green light just as the sun sets

Or as a shooting star in the dark night.
Filling the wholeness of my being,
Where beauty was hidden
Where enoughness resides
In a moment heart recognizes home.

—Trudy Gomez

For your day: *Allow yourself to be open to a moment when your heart leaps, says AH-HA, and recognizes that you are home with yourself, that you are enough.*

Day 46

Sometimes I mistake what I see for all there is until I recall that there's so much more that I don't see.

Fog of Unknowing

Alone, but never really alone.
Apparent moments of singularity
but still in communion with all that is.
Invisible only to the naked eye are
forces for good, angels constantly
surrounding us; working day and night
on our behalf through stories of our
telling and memories of our making,
breaking through our dreams and
breaking through our waking too.
Might we come to know that all
that is seen is not all there is.
In the fog of our unknowing
we will have only a given number
of days to penetrate the layers;
veil after veil, in search of a love
that was never lost, only temporarily
hidden from sight.

—Wendi Romero

For your day: *May I know that I am never alone.*

Day 47

Blind Faith

Mary our Mother,
Jesus' biological Mother.
I pray to you,
I ask for your intercession.
My days and nights
are consumed
by thoughts of my son,
his addiction issues.
I want help.
I need answers.
I wait.
Honestly,
I'm not liking the answer.
The problems aren't fixed.
I wait and pray.
God knows best.
He will give me peace.
I focus on Him,
trust Him.
This is the path
He has chosen for me.
I must stay focused.
God will guide me
in the right direction.
Blind faith.
Thank you, Mary my Mother.
Thank you, my Lord Jesus.

—Paula Simm

For your day: *Do you have a situation in which you could rely on your blind faith?*

Day 48

Pondering My Faith: Notes from My Life

Day 49

Healing What Is Broken

Day 50

What might I be willing to risk if not for the limitations I place on myself? What holds me back?

Broken Wing

It didn't stop the caterpillar
from crawling on its belly
nor did it keep it from
curling, not knowing that it
would hang upside down
for days in the dark.
It didn't stop the butterfly
from taking to flight
nor did it keep a clipped
wing from laboring against
a hard shell to break
through its long night.
Not knowing imperfection
or limitations, off it flew
broken wing and all.

—Wendi Romero

For your day: *May I exceed limits I place on myself today.*

Day 51

Relax

When we arrived home from St. Louis after my husband, Dee's, heart surgery, he still had much recuperating to do. His kidneys had been affected, and the doctors were hoping they would begin to heal themselves. The anxiety I had experienced in St. Louis did not go away.

I developed a burning pain in my left shoulder that massage and heat would not heal. Cortisone made me ill. I was taking ibuprofen daily and trying to find the answers to my pain.

My mind drifted back to my first massage many years before. When I walked in, overly stressed from my teaching job, the massage therapist said, "Oh, my. It looks like you are trying to cover your heart with your shoulders." As I remembered this, I knew I was doing this same thing; my shoulders, tense and tight, were curving forward, trying to cover an anxious heart.

My body was reacting to my mind, which was saying that Dee's recovery was up to me. Of course, it wasn't. I had little control over any facets of his health. I was almost carrying Dee around with me, figuratively speaking, and it was causing pain. I began to say to myself periodically, "Relax. God is in charge, not you. This isn't helping. Relax."

I discovered that I needed to bring this message to all areas of my life. It was truly hard for me to relax completely; I was always tensed and, "on go." And my body and mind were paying a price. Surrender was required. Letting go. Even—dare I say it—*giving up!* I had to give up my ideas of being in charge and become open to the Spirit. It was only when I practiced this several times a day, letting my shoulders relax, that my pain began to lessen.

This sort of letting go and relaxing is not the doorway to laziness or apathy but is instead a royal road to more health, serenity, and a deeper spirituality.

—Lyn Holley Doucet

For Your Day: *Relax, you are not in charge.*

Day 52

On our life's journey, there are many hills and valleys. Our invitation to transformation is continually coming to us in life's events. I tend to focus on the hard times but may benefit from the advice given so often: "just sit in the question."

The Broken Jar

Here sits a broken jar.
What use is it?
In past months, it was filled with a
swirling torrent of nourishing goodness.
Excitement, anticipation, and joyful acceptance
overflowed from its perfect form and usefulness.

Now all its life seems gone.
What is left—some brooding,
questioning, reluctance and
hesitancy to understand what happened?
It has a glimpse of how broken this jar is.

What are the questions for this broken jar to ask?
What is real and what is illusion?
What is leaking out?
Who can repair it?
What is there for it to do?

—Betty Landreneau

For your day: *Mourn your brokenness, give thanks for your brokenness, let go of your definition of usefulness.*

Day 53

Abandoned

These are the thoughts I wanted to share with my granddaughter as she anguished over her father's lack of involvement in her life.

As she suffered, I wanted to tell her this.

My beautiful girl, yes, your father loves you. But he knows not what he is doing to your hurting, tender heart as he was not shown this love.

Already, he left you and your mother because he doesn't yet realize the importance of fatherhood.

You've asked how he can abandon you in so many ways and you've said how it's your fault. But, it is not!!! It is a result of his brokenness, his confusion, his love of harmful things.

He probably has never heard that "a daughter's first love is her father." If he has, he doesn't understand this.

But you love him dearly. It doesn't matter what he has done, nor the many times hurt you. You forgive instantly when he gives you some attention.

You yearn longingly for him to acknowledge you, to attend your birthday parties, to bring you fun places, to buy you pretty clothes, to treat you as he does his other children, but he has seldom done any of these for you.

He hardly calls you. You've waited by the phone for his call and you're disappointed once more.

He promises, but hardly keeps those promises. "I'll help your mom get you some wheels and keep your oil changed. I will never leave you on foot!"

Those were the words that gave you hope of love and caring, but these were only more empty promises. My heart mourns for you. I want to scream at him, "How can you do this? How can you hurt your little girl, your first born? She should have been your little princess!"

You've told me you lie awake at night thinking about the way he treats you and you ask why you should care. How can he abandon you this way. I tell you it is not your fault. It's the way *he* wants his life! These are the choices *he* has made that keep him from you.

I hold you close, my firstborn grandchild, and I tell you there is a Father who loves you and has loved you even before you were born. He knows your pain. He knows how you feel abandoned. He loves you and He always will. He is always with you especially in others who love you, like your mom, your sisters, your brothers and your grandparents. Believe that! Feel that you are loved!

Always, He is with you! Always! Go to Him and He will heal your heart!

—Cheryl Delahoussaye.

For your day: *Do you know someone who feels alone or unloved by someone important in their lives? What would you tell them?*

Day 54

God appears in many different disguises, and healing can happen in odd places and unexpected ways.

More Than Skin Deep

The sun burns where I sit next to a glassed-in playground
of screaming kids. The line for food is long and winding,

but what really pulls me in is colored ink burned into skin.
Letters across knuckles, bodies reflecting what's carried

within. Names of children, living and lost, sacred hearts,
ex-wives, and lovers etched in flesh. My brother wears

a crown of thorns around his arm, and my cousin carries
a cross inscribed in the small of her back. People, places,

and things-no longer spoken of, finding a way to be said.
The day my father died, a part of my heart went with him;

a young woman bearing my name stamped on him like a
seal, an unbroken bond that even death could not diminish.

Tattoo removal ads are everywhere, but lasers can never
erase, nor cause us to forget what we carry deep inside.

There are many ways to speak.
There are many ways to heal.

—Wendi Romero

For your day: *May I be aware of God's healing no matter how it presents itself.*

Day 55

Healing What Is Broken: Notes from My Life

Day 56

Joy and Dancing

Art by Dana Manly

Day 57

In Lyn Holley Doucet's book Life on a River's Turning, her reflections on the spiritual life of a child describe the experiences of childhood that can "lead us forward into our destinies and the fruits that come from childhood joy and vulnerability."

My Life

In music and song You come to me,
filling my life with joy and leading me to praise You.
Many songs, now within me,
reveal a facet of Your Love and Light.
You have bound me to You by these rhythms.
Each one sings me into a new existence.

—Betty Landreneau

For your day: *Listen to your favorite songs. What are their messages to you?*

Day 58

I have been getting up during the night the last few nights because it is supposed to be the peak time to see meteor showers. I have been standing in the yard or lying on the chaise on the deck gazing into the night sky that is littered with stars. Today at centering prayer, some things synthesized for me: the readings, the song, the words shared. And what I have been experiencing and thinking about seemed to converge, and I was inspired to create.

Not long into meditation, the Holy Spirit, my muse—whatever you want to call the Voice that invades and does not go away until the words or pictures are put on paper—the voice persistently whispered, and this was the result:

Star Dancing

I move into the darkness and look up at the star-littered sky
On gentle night breeze
I hear a whispered invitation,
"Come dance with me."(Hafiz)
We'll dance the dance of outrageous joy;
the slow dance of gentle love.
We'll dance from light to light
from moment to moment
from hope to hope,
from peace to peace,
from joy to joy
We'll dance the dance of transformation
where there is no Me, no you, only One.

—Trudy Gomez

For your day: *How will I listen and respond when Spirit whispers in my ear?*

Day 59

I don't know which came first, these words or a painting that I did of birds soaring and sweeping through the sky. They have become intertwined in my memory.

The birds of the air do not worry
They swoop and soar
Carried by air currents
Just for the joy of it
Is that their passion?
They are free to just be birds
their purpose,
their nature.
To be true to my nature,
What is that?
How to do that?
What would that look like?
Not to contort my way of being
Not to conform to what is the expected
Not to bend and twist until I am unrecognizable
To live my purpose, my joy, my passion, my nature:
That is freedom!

—Trudy Gomez

For your day: *How will I live my passion today?*

Day 60

Dance with the Wild Child

The wild child has been invited to dance.
She looks around and remembers
she is called to be herself.
She doesn't even have to work at it
but simply relax into the Real You.

Advice from a sage was ever present in her mind:
"Your transformation is none of your business.
When it becomes a 'business' the ego directs the production."

So, for the wild child, the ever-present question,
"What am I to do?" is greeted with laughter.
Who told you, you were naked?
She knows her continued creation is full of surprises.
So, dance your dance, wild child.

"Dance, dance, wherever you may be
I am the lord of the dance, said he
And I lead you all, wherever you may be
And I lead you all in the dance, said he"
(Shaker melody, Lyrics by Sydney Carter)

—Betty Landreneau

For your day: *When were you invited to embrace your "wild child"?
What did it look like? Where in your body did you experience the
happiness of the wild child?*

Day 61

Soul is more expansive than either body or mind.
—David g. Benner

God at the Fais-Do-Do

One Sunday afternoon Dee and I went to hear Geno Delafose at a local club known for its Sunday afternoon dances. Geno Delafose is a celebrity Zydeco player, a cowboy in a hat and starched shirt, a genius on the piano accordion.

A crowd had gathered on the Henderson Lakes, in an old wooden building, and Dee and I were dancing. Well, I was dancing and Dee was kind-of-dancing. He was glad to take a seat when another gentleman invited me to the floor. By this time, the musical beat filled the space around us and pulsated with sounds and dancing feet and clapping hands. Twirling and spiraling, the rhythm was taking all of us to a different country.

The gentleman on the floor with me was an extremely good dancer, and I was thinking, *This is so much fun!* when suddenly time slowed and all my thinking was lifted up in bliss. I didn't know that dancing could be a religious experience; but I can tell you that, on this hot and humid August Sunday, I felt as if I were in church, as my soul was lifted, elated and joyful.

Scientists might explain this as *entrainment*, which happens when a group of people, animals, or even objects began to move together, in synch, on beat. It is an ancient joy, the heart of many religious festivals and rituals. I would say it is a gift of the soul: *we are all one.*

Around me that day were all sorts of people from all walks of life, and each of us was celebrating life. Experiencing happiness. Sharing a space without any malice or judgment and being ourselves. Surely this was holy.

As Dee and I left the club, I saw the gentleman from my dance. He said to me with a smile, "You're a good dancer." Well, that was just a bit of icing on a sweet and soulful dessert.

—Lyn Holley Doucet

For your day: *When and where have I experienced God in unexpected places?*

Day 62

Joy and Dancing: Notes from My Life

Day 63

Holy Feminine

Day 64

Sorrowful, yet always rejoicing. Poor but we give spiritual riches to others. We own nothing and yet possess everything.
—2 Corinthians 6:10

Happy Woman's Day

As I'm writing this, it's Mother's Day weekend. I am not only in prayer for all those women who have children, but also my heart is heavy for all the women who don't have children but desperately want them. My heart is heavy for all those mothers who had children but have lost them, whether through death, kidnapping, drugs, or just lack of communication. Sad to say, but there are many. We, as women, regardless of our circumstances, have pretty much the same feelings and questions.

There is joy and pain in all situations. When thinking of mothers, of course, my first thought is of Mary, mother of Jesus. Joy and pain she most definitely felt, but she wouldn't have had it any other way. She was a woman of compassion and a mother of sorrows. And so Mary, having suffered and overcome so much, can help all women on their journeys. A woman wanting children, the woman who has lost her child—each has compassion and a heart filled with sorrows, and each, not understanding, asks "Why?" All women ponder life experiences, pray about them, stand in the mystery of life, trying to figure out, "What is the lesson in all of this?"

My own mother experienced joy and pain with me. I was a wounded child because of so many issues and circumstances she had absolutely no control over and was not aware of. It was not until I was an adult that I was strong enough to break my silence, only when I was ready.

The one thing she always did was love me unconditionally, which helped pull me through those dark times. Finally, joy has come, and I am honored to be with her. But she asked, "Why would my daughter have to go through such dark times?"

I too experienced joy and pain with my step-son, who at age eighteen went home to our Heavenly Father due to an accident one month after his high-school graduation. I have learned to live with the loss. I felt joy the short time he was here, but he is always with me. I ask, "Why?"

I look at my own daughter now, a mother, doing a beautiful job raising her two girls. As in life, she will experience her own joy and pain with them, and she will be better prepared because of her own experiences of loss.

So, I just want to shout out, "Happy Woman's Day!" with hope and strength for all, in whatever your situation this day. I pray that I might be a vehicle of light, giving thanks for the joy and the pain. I trust we are all healing, even when we don't have the answer, just yet, to the "whys?"

—Denise Broussard

For your day: *When there is sorrow in life and we don't know why, how can we trust that we will feel joy in our heart?*

Day 65

But Mary stayed outside the tomb weeping. And as she wept, she bent over into the tomb and saw two angels in white sitting there, one at the head and one at the feet where the body of Jesus had been. And they said to her, "Woman, why are you weeping?" She said to them, "They have taken my Lord, and I don't know where they laid him." When she had said this, she turned around and saw Jesus there, but did not know it was Jesus. Jesus said to her, "Woman, why are you weeping? Whom are you looking for?" She thought it was the gardener and said to him, "Sir, if you carried him away, tell me where you laid him, and I will take him." Jesus said to her, "Mary!" She turned and said to him in Hebrew, "Rabbouni," which means Teacher. Jesus said to her, "Stop holding on to me for I have not yet ascended to the Father. But go to my brothers and tell them, 'I am going to my Father and your Father, to my God and your God.' "Mary of Magdala went and announced to the disciples, "I have seen the Lord," and what he told her.
—John 20:11-18

The Gospels for the Easter Vigil, Easter Sunday, and the Monday and Tuesday of the Octave of Easter have all started with Mary Magdalene's encounter with the empty tomb and the risen Jesus. When I read these Gospels, I wonder how it is that women are still relegated to the sidelines. A woman was the Christ-bearer, a woman was the first to encounter the risen Lord, the first to recognize and proclaim that Jesus has overcome the grave, and the first to proclaim his message to the apostles.

The early church did have women in major roles; they presided over home churches, taught, and preached. They did not just play a supporting role to the men of the church. I know cultural mores had a lot to do with the roles of women, but wasn't the early church counter-cultural? Wasn't Jesus counter-cultural? Isn't that what today's church should be?

Isn't the church, the institution and the people, supposed to have that same role today? Isn't church supposed to stand up for the truth of Christ, to proclaim that truth; to not be concerned with style and form over truth? Ritual and rules are important, but what is more important the letter of the law or the spirit of the law? Aren't the promises of God more important than guarding turf and form and style rather than proclaiming the truth?

We are temples of the Holy Spirit, and when we accept this concept we also accept that we are blessed with the gifts of the Spirit and that we are expected to use those gifts. God gave us a brain and a free will, and we are meant to exercise them. We are to search out truth as Mary searched out the empty tomb. We are to see for ourselves, to use discernment, to give form to truth. We are to gather knowledge, to seek wisdom, to pray for guidance and enlightenment, to have informed consciences. Otherwise how can we be true servants? How else can we be proclaimers of the Risen Lord and not just cultic, mindless followers?

—Trudy Gomez

For your day: *How will I be a discerning witness to the Risen Lord?*

Day 66

Great Mother

O Great Mother, your gentle embrace
gives me courage to be open to the
onslaught of your Love.
The River of Acceptance flowing
through You into me
fills my heart with a sweet aching
to let you do with me as you will.
Your desire for me is stronger than
my effort to be independent, in control,
to hold myself apart from you—
hoping to be better, worthy, more "put together."
Instead, today I open my brokenness
to your loving gaze.
I offer the me I am today and know
I am enough.
Praise and glory be to You,
O Great Mother, for your
gift of me to myself.

—Betty Landreneau

For your day: *Today I love myself as You love me.*

Day 67

As the first day of the week was dawning Mary Magdalene and the other Mary came to see the tomb. ... And behold, Jesus met them on their way and greeted them. They approached, embraced his feet, and did him homage. Then Jesus said to them, "Do not be afraid. Go tell my brothers to go to Galilee, and there they will see me."
—Matthew 28:8-10

In Matthew's Gospel, the Marys ran from the tomb "fearful yet overjoyed." Did they know that Jesus was resurrected, or had they been mistaken? Was He not dead? Had He managed to escape the tomb? But then they met the resurrected Jesus! He himself clarified it for them.

These women were the heralds, the first witnesses to the resurrected Christ. However, because they were women, the testimony was not considered legal. Women had no status in those times. The men did the job of spreading the Gospel, but without women, I don't think that Christianity could have survived. We, as women, in most cases, are the first teachers and nurturers of faith.

In societies today, the voices of women are being silenced. We see this especially in the Middle East and Africa. We see the UN appointing countries who oppress women to the council dealing with the rights of women ... corruption seems to abound everywhere.

—Trudy Gomez

For your day: *Today I will pray for the voiceless and the oppressed.*

Day 68

Mary took a pound of costly ointment of pure nard and anointed the feet of Jesus and wiped his feet with her hair; and the house was filled with the fragrance of the ointment. ... But Judas said, "Why was this ointment not sold?"
—John 12:1-8

On the way to the cross is an unexpected detour that prefigures the pouring out of love at a cost that is priceless. A plan laid out before time immemorial filled with such extravagant love that we can't wrap our minds around it.

Mary demonstrates extravagant love; Mary who lets down her hair in public and anoints the feet of the Lord, the feet at which she sat in earlier Gospel stories. There is an intimate sort of love being poured out, a passionate love, a love that takes risks—women did not expose their unbound hair to anyone but their husbands. It is love that cannot and will not be hidden, a submissive love demonstrated through Mary's actions.

We are perhaps like Judas in that we see only the surface. We don't or can't grasp the free and extravagant gift. It may not be because we are stingy with our love. It may be that we can't comprehend such love and we may be incapable of such love because we are bound by our human condition. The way we know love does not match up with the way Love knows love.

I think we all hold something back when it comes to love because we fear being hurt or rejected: self-protection. We look at Jesus. He poured out love, and he was rejected by many, so what chance do we have at matching such love? Jesus knew the risk and he went ahead with the Father's plan. He held nothing back!

—Trudy Gomez

For your day: *How will I love extravagantly today?*

Day 69

Holy Feminine: Notes from My Life

Day 70

Birthing Times

Photo by Patty Prather

Day 71

One body and one Spirit, as you were also called to the one hope of your call; one Lord, one faith, one baptism; one God and Father of all, who is over all and through all and in all.
—Ephesians 4:4-6

Be Made New

In the waters of new birth
I am caressed, upheld
lifted above this earthen shell to a higher place.
It is open, fresh, clean.
A new beginning.

In the waters of new birth
spirit teems in its depths
whispering secrets of freedom.
If only I believe. If only I allow.

Inhale deeply.
Accept it as it is—a gift from God.
Breathe out all doubt. Believe.
Be the person you were meant to be!

—Velma LeBlanc Cheramie

For your day: *Remember the gifts of God that have brought you new life. How did this gift come about? Journal about your experience.*

Day 72

I have called you by name. You are mine.
—Isaiah 43:1

NO NAME

"By name I have called you,

You are precious to me."

I sing the phrase once again.

"By name I have called you…"

My conscious begins to float through my synapses, desperately rooting for names of my ancestors Lynch, Calloway, Kerby, Sylvester, Oma, Marian, George, Joseph—and then a blank slate.

Only these ancestors' names remain etched in the recesses of my memory from the written and oral tradition. I know some random facts about them, but I do not know their life stories. What were their dreams for the future generations of their descendants?

Did they even have time to ponder what life would be like for those that would continue to fill the empty branches of their family tree, or were the hours in their days consumed with daily survival?

In less than five generations, will the same be said about me? The dreams I have for those that follow will never be expressed. Even *ancestry.com* will not be able to answer the esoteric questions of family seekers trying to connect the dots. The seekers might see a photo or a video of me, but none of the seekers will be able to ask a direct question of me. They will have knowledge of my life, but factual knowledge fails to breathe an emotional connection. My descendants in five generations will never experience an empty space in their lives from having known me.

In five generations human beings who are my direct descendants will not recall my name. So why the emphasis on naming a human?

Man tried to name their creator and the creator said, "My name is I am." In the realm of the universe I am not even counted as being as noticeable as one grain of sand. And yet, my God has called me by name.

In the stillness I hear Him calling each of His creatures, His beloved. He calls me to Himself, of this I am certain. And it matters not that in five generations the mention of my name will not even bring a recognition to any human who walks the earth.

The only thing that matters, as I live this gift of life, is the knowledge that I was created by my Maker, "I AM", to leave traces of His love, so that others may be open to hearing Him whisper, "Do not be afraid, you were made by Me to Love you into Love."

—Patty Prather

For your day: *Read 1 Corinthians 13: 4-6 and replace the word Love with your given name.*

Day 73

What are you creating/birthing/blessing into the world?
—Amber Kuileimailani Bonnici

The feeling that came to me as I read the phrase blessing into the world was one of wonder and then of recognition that there might be a greater purpose for the creations that birth within me than I have previously considered. I have never thought about blessing outward as being a part of the creative/ birthing process. How lovely I find the concept, and how true it is. I find myself pulled into a place of grace and openness as I love a creation into existence. How can that not be a blessing?

I think of all the mentors I know through their creative works and written words, and I am blessed. Mentors have blessed me doubly by their creations and their friendship.

We speak of birthing our ideas and creations when we are giving life to them, and the creation process is, many times, one of carrying, holding, and feeding. I now recognize that there is a blessing component to creative efforts, a prayer offered for the gestation and birth of this sacred act of creation that moves out from our single self.

I have always had something creative in the works, as many of us do, and I find that, when I am in the space with whatever art I am creating, I experience real enjoyment and care through the process. I love when my creations go out into the world for the appreciation of others. I have loved some of my creative endeavors so greatly that I am certain blessings went out from them even if no one else ever saw them. My love of them was all that was necessary to create a blessing. I often say, "I am having so much fun with this." What a blessing fun is! Creative joy is God given, a blessing in the world.

—Avis Lyons LeBlanc

For your day: *How can you acknowledge the blessings your creations offer?*

Day 74

I Am Not a Tree

One late spring afternoon, a tiny life entered my world. For what seemed like days, I watched him. Amazed that this baby boy with blonde hair, dimples, tiny fingers and toes lived and grew within me, I felt a shift, a weight. I cried the day mama left. She showed me how to love, how to mother, how to protect, but now I was on my own.

Twenty-seven years later, as I sit and reflect about the life of my beautiful son and daughter, I am filled with love, pride, regret, loss, happiness, and hope. My hands, now aging, look like Mama's and I feel comforted by this. My heart is full, appreciates her love but also the loss she experienced. What must she have felt when her children turned and walked away. My heart knows this sting as I try to cling no more.

Poet Mark Nepo is quoted as saying *"I envy the tree, how it reaches but never holds."* I think we are all meant to hold, and then we are meant to let go. But how? I am not a tree. I guess this letting go is a dance we all grow to love and hate, but a dance we can't sit out. I hold tight, until it is time. Just as my next breath is a reflex, holding is as well. As I try to hold my children close, today I take a lesson from the tree. Just as their branches reach to the sun, I too, will do my best to reach. I will lift what were once my babies in prayer to the One who loves them more than I do. And one day, as they parent their own, they may feel the loss of me, and the circle of life shall go on.

—Jane DeBlieux

For your day*: To what do you cling? Always remember that we are unable to receive if our fists are clenched forever. Slowly release, in order to receive.*

Day 75

When I find myself at a crossroads, I often withdraw to an out-of-the-way place. This gives me a different perspective, a wider vantage point.

Fertile Ground

Every once in awhile
I withdraw from my familiar.
I lie on my back and watch
clouds go by, or head out
for a long quiet drive.
Not all things are able
to grow in one spot,
so sometimes I set my sight
on somewhere else.
It often takes bravery
and the risk of my utter
aloneness to seek out
that unknown patch of
fertile ground where only
I was meant to blossom.

—Wendi Romero

For your day: *May I find my fertile ground.*

Day 76

Birthing Times: Notes from My Life

Day 77

Blessed Encounters

Day 78

The Ship in the Shipyard

When my daughter was living and working in New Orleans, we would walk to a little neighborhood chapel near her house; it didn't seat more than 50 or so folks comfortably. We attended Mass on Mother's Day weekend, and the Gospel reading was about the sheep and the shepherd (John 10:1-10).

The priest was Asian and spoke with a heavy accent. As he was reading the Gospel, my daughter leaned over and said, *This is a reading I've never heard before!* She must have seen my puzzled look because she clarified, *You know, about the ship and the shipyard.* I couldn't help but laugh. Because of the priest's accent, instead of sheep and the shepherd, she heard "ship in shipyard."

She had gotten excited because she thought she was hearing something new; a new Gospel story.

It could be a Gospel story about the sheltered place where we are formed and built and fortified and perfected and made ready for sailing. It could be about a safe harbor where we are refurbished, where the barnacles that we have accumulated are scraped off, where the rotten wood is replaced, where the leaks are fixed, our sails are mended, and so on with the metaphors or parables.

Too bad we can't be excited every time we hear the good news. What if we could hear with new ears and new insights?

I still smile whenever I hear the Gospel of the *Ship and the Shipyard.*

—Trudy Gomez

For your day: *When was the last time you were excited by the Word of God?*

Day 79

Before I formed you in the womb, I knew you. Before you were born I set you apart.
—Jeremiah 1:5

Loved from all Time

On an evening in 1999, I arrived in Grand Coteau for my second retreat. I believed I had put most of the pain behind me that I had long struggled with, pain arising from a history of sexual abuse and deaths of loved ones and friends, starting when I was quite young. Therapy and spiritual direction had helped me heal and to forgive my abusers. I do know this now: I will continue to make peace with my youth until I meet my Maker, but I don't have to do it alone.

The first day of retreat began with much anticipation and joy, but I struggled to participate because I kept crying, which I couldn't understand. I immediately started asking, "Lord, what are you trying to show me? What is happening to me?" I felt something stirring. I continued attending the talks, sought guidance through scripture and prayer, and journaled during my quiet times. I lay down for a nap and was awakened, with God revealing to me, in a way I could understand, that I was mourning my biological father, whom I never really knew. He was never a part of my life, and I loved my step-father, who had been my dad all along. But God was revealing to me that I had covered the hurt of feeling abandoned my entire life, and it was time to heal. I didn't think I had any feelings about my biological father, never suspected that he disturbed me at all.

I realized that, in my mother's womb from the time of conception, I believed I had been abandoned. It impacted my behavior in negative ways, causing depression, addictions, and unhealthy behavior.

A friend, who had no idea what I was experiencing in my room, had slipped a children's book under my door. I noticed it and picked it up as I was leaving to get some air and hopefully sit and swing under a tree. The name of the book was *On the Day you were Born*. This tells how all God's creation celebrates when a baby comes into the world. Through this answered prayer, I realized that God celebrated on the day I was conceived and that, on the day I was born, all God's creation was glad I was here.

The last day of the retreat, a young woman came to share with me before departing, that while I was swinging under the tree, reading that book, the rays of the sun were shining through the branches, and it looked to her like God's arms were wrapped around me, holding me. She had no idea what had transpired in my room, but that's exactly how I felt.

I left that last day, knowing I had to forgive my biological father, and God let me know, loud and clear, that I am never alone, and He will always love me, no matter what. Just another step toward peace in my heart.

—Denise Broussard

For your day: *Can you take your pain and suffering into silence to find the healing love of our Lord?*

Day 80

You change your life by changing your heart.
— Max Lucado

The Man in the Plaid Shirt

We sat within the expanse of cafeteria tables. I sat slouched on a cold folding chair on one side of the table. Directly across from me sat a man in a plaid shirt. The table between us, clear of any sign of life, lay bare and waiting.

His day old beard was as scruffy as a brillo pad and his deep set eyes were the color of blue marbles. I did not yet know that this stranger would be a savior in my life.

Some might call it a born again experience. I call it freedom!

Amid a profound silence the man in the plaid shirt spoke softly of his pain and of the pain he had caused others. His words were like shards of broken glass as they scattered across the once empty space between us. I saw myself reflected in the broken pieces.

I recalled images of my life and I realized that every decision I had made, prior to this time, was shrouded by the F-O-G. I emerged from this brokenness to a realization that I had lived my entire life in a F-O-G. Now the F-O-G was lifted.

F for fear. Fear of rejection. Fear of being judged. I became a people pleaser.

O for obligation. How many decisions had I made through feeling obligated?

G for guilt. When presented with a situation, how often had guilt made me say "Yes," when "No" would better serve?

On an ordinary Monday, a man whose name I would never know changed the way I had been living since I first reached consciousness.

I don't remember the date but I will always remember how I felt after hearing this stranger's life story, it created a huge shift in my soul.

I left the cafeteria that day and went directly to visit someone whose visits in the past had always left me depressed. Because, prior to this visit I was driven by all three of my demons; fear, obligation and guilt.

The F-O-G lifted that day. I realized my future was to center all my decisions from a place of love. I was going because of love, and only to love, for the broken human waiting for my visit.

Now, when God presents me with another's needs or requests, or when I am asked for something I may not feel called to, I stop and reflect, and I examine my choices. I remind myself to not act on the request if F-O-G shrouds my soul.

Love and only love is my motivation. Otherwise, I have fallen into the dense fog of my previous life.

My life is forever changed by the man in the plaid shirt who shared his message about how to live life through love, even in our darkest moments.

—Patty Prather

For your day: *Our lives reflect our beliefs. What are you choosing today?*

Day 81

God gives us daily gifts we do not recognize and so I pray, "let me be truly present in each waking hour".

The Woman I Never Knew

I could see her smile a block away.

There was never a day when there was no smile.

The only differences I ever noted were changes in her attire.

Some days she was dressed in a housecoat and slippers with her white hair tightly rolled up in curlers.The bristles leaving pink marks in her scalp.

Other times she was dressed as if she was going to meet friends to play bridge or share a lunch.

She was a constant on my daily walk.

I could always count on passing her as I walked my dog and she chased after her little dog, Frankie.

One day I noticed she was wearing a kerchief and had lost her hair.

We stopped and chatted as she told me of her cancer diagnosis.

I told her how sorry I was and that I would be praying for her as she walked the long suffering road to a possible cure.

I had noticed she had a distinct accent but never deciphered where its origins were from and never spoke to her longer than five minutes.

I saw this woman almost every day of my life for at least eight years as I walked my dog.

Most of the time we just smiled at one another, or both of us spent time trying to round up our dogs that were let free of their bonds of obedience when our paths crossed and they frolicked together.

I tend to know the names of the dogs on my path more than the humans and for this I am sorry.

One morning I saw her obituary in the newspaper and began to weep for the stranger I never knew.

I spent months grieving her, even though I never really knew her. She was someone familiar to me in my everyday life. Like the postman or the check out clerk or the bus driver.

I believe part of my grief was for what I missed in not really knowing her.

Her obit spoke of her love of music and how she had survived in Poland during WWII and had lost so many family members in the concentration camps. She was a chemist. She loved singing and she loved America. And in the end her ashes were being brought back to her homeland to be buried with her husband in Poland.

I am left with a deep hole for the opportunity I missed to have truly known such a beautiful soul.

—Patty Prather

For your day: *How many people do you pass on a daily basis that you would miss if they are no longer here? Choose someone you see and get to know them a little better.*

Day 82

Messenger

I have heard friends speak about their furry friends as messengers from God. I have had many pets in my life, from living on a dairy farm to adopting grandpuppies when my son's and daughter's lives changed. These days, my furry friend is a boxer I saved in 2011 during a cold, rainy storm. I found her under the steps of our deck, shivering and bleeding. I could see she was female, so I called her, "Girl, Girl, Girl!" and she finally came to me so I could help her. I became her master, and she became my Girl.

These are messages I've received from Girl:
Believe my Master will always provide for my every need.
Allow my Master to heal an ailing heart. (Not long after I saved her, she had to have a heartworm treatment.)
Eat the nourishing food my Master provides.
Allow my master to hold me when I shiver with fear, and relax in my Master's arms.
Let my Master apply the ointment of healing when I am wounded by life's troubles.
Show loved ones I have missed them while they were gone. Kiss them! Jump for Joy!
Be wiggly excited and bouncing happy when they return home.
Run and run and run, freely and very often!
Take the time for adventure on a perfectly bright sunny day provided from above, and frolic in the fresh, green grass. Catch a Frisbee thrown by a loved one and feel the cool breeze on my cheeks.
Enjoy simply sitting with loved ones, listening to them and appreciating them with my whole being.

Explore anything (especially my heart) but beware of skunks! (Yes! One evening she was sprayed by a mother skunk that was searching for food for her babies!)
Adore my Master always!

—Cheryl Delahoussaye

For your day: *Have you had a pet inspire you in meditation? Where or when do you find the arms of the Master waiting for you?*

Day 83

Blessed Encounters: Notes from My Life

Day 84

Spiritual Friendship

Photo by Jill Duhon

Day 85

As women, we search for community; a place in which we can share our spiritual journeys and all our feelings. It is so freeing to come as we are and find ourselves accepted. Consider whether you have found this place for yourself, or are still longing for those sorts of spiritual sisters. God hears your prayer.

Lead Me

lead me
to a place of love
one of trust
where joy is shared
and pain, as well

lead me
to those who search
for meaning
who thirst for more
who question
and challenge

lead me
to a place of acceptance
where eyes see
but never judge
where words guide
but do not cut
where hearts beat safely
with unrestrained love

lead me
to a place of hope
where dreams are fed
and wounds are healed

a place of peace
where the quiet is your heart
and your breath is my voice

—Jane DeBlieux

For your day: *Lead me to sisters of the heart.*

Day 86

The soul longs for the greatest of all blessings that the divine nature can accomplish. This is that the divine nature should bring itself forward and accomplish a comparison of the soul with itself, that is, with the divine nature. The greatest blessing on heaven and earth is based on equality.
—Meister Eckhard

The Greatest of All Blessings

I sat in prayer with the group on a Thursday morning. I could hear the birds singing outside, the mew of Maddie the cat. Inside the little house, there was breath and silence and movement of energy. I had this deep insight: When my eyes are closed and I can't see that others have separate bodies, we feel like one body. I also asked myself, *Is this the kingdom of God? That all might be one? Is this, as well, what it is like to enter death's door? That I lose myself in the oneness of Spirit?*

It doesn't seem so earth-shattering as I write it. The energy lay in the deep experience of oneness, the absolute equality of spirits that make up the one God. Somehow even the birds had moved into me; their lilting song was part of me, part of us all. It was only in the silence that I could glimpse this. It was only in the quiet that the divine nature put itself forward and saturated my soul.

—Lyn Holley Doucet

For your day: *We are one.*

Day 87

"For where two or three are gathered together in my name, there am I in the midst of them."
—*Matthew 18:20*
"A faithful friend is a sturdy shelter; he who finds one finds a treasure." Sirach 6:14
"... out of weakness they were made powerful" —2 Corinthians: 34

Pinky Link

I had to laugh at myself as I read something from one of my journals because it was nonsensical. I am sharing it with you in spite of its silliness because there is a modicum of wisdom in it ... not my wisdom but a gift of the Spirit.

Journal Date December 19, 2006

While I was sitting in prayer an idea came to me about humanity. I'm not sure why this came up.
We are all weak. I was praying that God would forgive me for my selfishness, jealousy, pride and always having to be right. I want to serve Him through my neighbors and my family, but I find myself getting resentful and feeling reluctant. What a paradox! What do I do with that? It is so frustrating that I am so weak and selfish.
Are you weak my neighbor, my friend? For whatever reason, I thought of my little finger, the pinky. It's pretty useless, right?! I cannot think of anything I can accomplish with my pinky. I can decorate it with a ring. I can tie a string or ribbon on it as a reminder.

I look to you, my sister, my friend and I ask: do you have weaknesses like me? If you do, could you pray for me in my weaknesses? I really need help or at least support. Would you say a little prayer for me as I say a prayer for you? If we link up at our weakest points, maybe it will make us stronger in Christ because where two or three gather in His name, He is there.

Pinky Link! This is nuts!! Aye?

—Velma LeBlanc Cheramie

For your day: *Link up today with someone who will lift your spirits and help you remember to believe in yourself. God loves you.*

Day 88

We have all known the long loneliness, and we have found that the answer is community.
—*Dorothy Day*

Community

Possibilities nurtured,
accepted, explored.
Precious,
irreplaceable,
beyond price.

Where thoughts,
shared with other
thoughtful, caring persons
can rise
to an understanding
uplifted by the sharing.

My singular ideas,
explored with others,
with intentionality,
ripen into
more seasoned plans.

Where laughter,
joined with
others' laughter,
flings great joy
out into the world.

Where love,
compounded with
the love of many,
sends greater

love to where
love is needed.

Tears and grief
shared with others
who validate
and honor
one's path of sadness
supports healing.

Being together
in silence,
with others
within their silence,
creates trust
and safety
sending
a more peaceful
person into the world.

—Avis Lyons LeBlanc
For your day: *Participate in community where you find it. Be one who helps develop it along its path.*

Day 89

To discover a kindred spirit is to find your heart in the heart of a friend.
—Ann Parrish

Honeysuckle Cottage

From the outside, the cottage could be mistaken for a tool shed. It is a tool shed but not the kind for garden supplies and tools. It is a tool shed for the seekers.

A friend knew I was searching for such a sanctuary and had been going to Sacred Center for a year. She would still find time to meet for meditative prayer with a friend and me twice a month. The three of us were hungry to be part of a community that was open to all pathways to God. A community where we could be our authentic selves and share our deepest questions, experiences, doubts and beliefs with no fear of judgement. The three of us needed more than just each other and so my friend, Pat, asked us if we would like to pray one day at Sacred Center. She told us that Lyn Doucet had opened her heart and her little cottage to what has evolved into Sacred Center.

I will be forever grateful that Lyn answered the call to simply ask others to meet for prayer.

So with an open heart and mild trepidation, I imagined crossing the threshold of a cottage full of women I had never met. I whispered a prayer of thanksgiving for all who were present behind the door.

As I walked the garden path to the Tool Shed, I noticed a plaque that hangs on the cottage door with the words "Honeysuckle Cottage."

Honeysuckles prefer full sun; they will tolerate some shade but they are "into" full sun! I like that!

I was brought back to a childhood memory of pulling off the honeysuckle flowers and sucking the nectar. The smell of honeysuckle today rates right up there with fresh mowed spring grass with wild onions.

I became like an excited hummingbird diving for the sip of nectar to become closer to my Creator.

I had spent years looking for sisters that would meet regularly throughout the entire year to support one another on their spiritual journey in an open non-scripted format. One where each brought her own unique gifts and shared her life's journeys and the different ways God drew them into closer relationship with Him.

Well, what a surprise! Little did I know that I was walking onto the holiest ground in South Louisiana in little old Maurice, Louisiana in a 10 by 12 foot cottage with no bathroom that sometimes holds as many as sixteen women of varying ages on any given Thursday morning.

Each woman offers me new tools in planting new seeds of spiritual growth. They have become gardeners of my soul, tilling the moist soil ready for planting, encouraging me to grow, watering the parched earth when I cannot find even one seed in the ashes of my life, sharing from the depths of their souls what helped them through the darkest hours, and lest you think it is all deep and serious, there is always an abundance of laughter in our midst.

We are artists, mothers, authors, wives, healers, singles, all women answering the call of all seekers. We are a Sacred Center.

—Patty Prather

For your day: *Ponder the value of all the small communities you are a part of and how each makes a difference in your life. Then offer a prayer of gratitude.*

Day 90

Spiritual Friendship: Notes from My Life

Day 91

Christ Among Us

Day 92

This is the day the lord has made; we will rejoice and be glad in it.
—Psalm 118:24

Keeping it Simple Today

I arise today
grateful for each single moment.
Safe trip to a white sandy beach and clear blue sky and water,
watching the sunset!
To be with my children and grandchildren,
listening to music, tasting good food & drink.
A soft bed and pillow to lay and rest.
For the lightening show during the night.
To hear the roar of the thunder.
Listening to the rain pound the glass.
Waking up to a glorious morning.
Watching the sunrise for a new day.
Drinking that first cup of coffee.
Ears in tune to the sound of little voices asking "Where's Pop?
Where's Neesy? Where's Uncle Smitty?"
All with Christ before me, behind me, below me, to my right, to
my left, and beside me!
Keeping it simple today, just Loving!

—Denise Broussard

For your day: *Can we, from day to day, become more aware of living
one moment at a time simply loving?*

Day 93

He called a little child to him, and placed the child among them.
And he said, "Truly, I tell you, unless you change and become
like little children, you will never enter the kingdom of heaven.
Therefore, whoever takes the low position of this child is the
greatest in the kingdom of heaven."
—Matthew 18:2-4

One Question

Every Advent when my children were young, we gathered around the
Advent wreath. In the middle of the wreath sat a very simple wooden
angel with broad carved wings.

We always began our Advent prayer time singing a sweet song entitled
"Light the Advent Candle" by Mary Lu Walker. Each week a new
verse was added as the next candle was lit. The chorus lyrics are:
Candle, candle burning bright
Shining in the cold winter night
Candle, candle burning bright
Fill our hearts with Christmas light.

I can close my eyes and vividly recall my young family sitting in
our darkened living room with only the light from the candles on the
Advent wreath.

After lighting the wreath, we would go around our circle, giving
thanks for each of our unique blessings that occurred on that day.
After a round of thanksgiving, a question was asked for each of us to
ponder in the cold night as the light from the wreath flickered across
our faces. One by one, we would go around the circle taking turns
sharing what feelings or thoughts that question evoked in us.

One night the question was, "When you get to heaven if you could
ask God only one question what would you ask Him?"

The sharing of answers to this question just happened to be from the
eldest to the youngest in our family that particular night.

Little did I know that it would change my spiritual life forever.
The questions that came up were, "Why is there suffering in the world?"
"Why didn't you cure my dear friend who died at age six from cancer?"
"What existed before the creation of the universe?"

The last to share his question was the baby of the family.
He was eight or nine years old. His response still takes my breath away.

In the darkness on a cold winter night, surrounded by the love of family, he spoke these words that silenced us:
"If I had only ONE QUESTION, I would ask, Can I kiss your wounds to thank you?"

—Patty Prather

For your day: *What rituals do you practice in your spiritual life?*
If you had but One Question to ask God today, what would it be?

Day 94

Jesus took Peter, James, and John and led them up a high mountain apart by themselves. And he was transfigured before them. . . . As they were coming down from the mountain, he charged them not to relate what they had seen to anyone.
— Mark 9:2-9

The Transfiguration of the Lord

After their mountaintop experience, Peter, James, and John pondered it and discussed it among themselves. They had a glimpse of Jesus' glory but also had been told that Jesus would suffer, die, and be resurrected. What did that mean? It was a lot to think and wonder about. They were told to keep to themselves what they had seen.

Could I have kept such an experience a secret?

Sometimes I think I get a glimpse of Jesus' glory: something in nature, or during Mass while receiving Eucharist. During those times, it is easy to say Yes; I have seen the truth of Jesus. But to actually internalize it, to conform my life to it, to allow myself to be transformed by that truth, is far more difficult.

Like the three apostles after their mountaintop experience, I continue to ponder Truth and strive to understand and live in a way that brings me closer to Truth. Some days are better than others. Sometimes I get it, other times, well . . .

—Trudy Gomez

For your day: *How do you see God's light in your life?*

Day 95

The Well

Weaving in and out, I avoid them
their stares, their taunts, their cutting tongues.
I choose to take the long way,
stones cutting my feet as the sun beamed high and hot.
Oh, but for a moment of shade, a moment of rest.

There will be no one there, so I push on,
making my way, hiding beneath my heavy robe.
I'm suddenly afraid.
Why did I do this?
I don't know, maybe I don't care anymore
maybe they are right;
maybe I am not good enough to be with them,
yet I am here.

And finally here it is: the well,
standing alone in the distance
as if daring me to approach.
Shuffling my feet in the dust
eyes focused, I slowly approach.
I hear the laughter, my cue to run.
Slowly, the familiar feeling consumes me
like a vine squeezing me lifeless.
I feel sick.
Much smaller now, I rush to fill my jug.
Without a word
I feel a presence
and then – a voice
may I trouble you for some water?

Didn't he hear the laughter?
Doesn't he *know*?
Afraid to look up, I stare at his dusty feet,
and again, he asks,
the water . . .may I share some of your water?

As if sensing my fear, he takes his finger
and slowly lifts my chin.
Looking into his eyes, I see tears.
But why?
Why does he have tears in his eyes?
Suddenly I realize
he knows.
He looks into me with a pierced knowing,
and He cries,
he cries for me.

I slowly serve him, and as he drinks I wonder
who is this man who has made it all right
for me to be me?

—Jane DeBlieux

For your day: *Are you afraid to approach the well in your life?*
Imagine Jesus encouraging you to be yourself. What might his words
to you be?

Day 96

Holy Communion

Fasting during Lent from the daily routine of celebrating the Eucharistic liturgy seemed like the wrong thing to do. What was it that made that decision seem like the right thing to do this year?

Without trying to justify this new Lenten practice, I reflected on how much these celebrations meant to me in the past. I thought of the thousands of times I received Holy Communion in the context of the liturgical rite. Has this encounter been transforming my behavior? Does this Bread of Life give me the "energy boost" needed to be more aware of Christ acting in and through me? Has it become so ordinary that I am like an automaton? What would make me a better conduit for the Christ-life?

Something or someone moved me to abstain from this daily celebration, and I began to notice the other holy encounters occurring each day. With surprising regularity, I was aware of moments of holy communion with people I encountered in everyday activities and in the wonders of nature. I was invited in the simple ordinary moments to be present, to listen to or assist another person or just be open to a new experience. These encounters became for me moments of awakening to the Spirit working in my world.

In the call to be myself and allow the Christ-life to flow through me in love and service, my recognition of our Oneness surprised me each time it happened. By saying yes to this invitation to be present and allow myself to participate in life, I can become the Light of the world, the salt of the earth, the city set on the mountaintop. I cannot do this alone, but only by embracing my communion with this body of Christ. Through Him, with Him and in Him, as Sue Monk Kidd says on page 56 of her book, *When the Heart Waits,* "we are scripts written collectively", telling the story of Love, giving to the world the evidence of our holy communion.

—Betty Landreneau

For your day: *Reflect on the attention you give to celebrating the sacraments. How can you do these actions with more awareness?*

Day 97

Christ Among Us: Notes from My Life

Day 98

Times to Mourn

Photo by Denise Broussard

Day 99

Doth a fountain send forth at the same place sweet water and bitter?
—James 3:11

Bittersweet: an Advent Reflection

My feelings right now are bittersweet. This is my favorite time of the year, waiting, with anticipation, for the great love, Jesus, to be born. I ponder Mary and her saying yes to the great mystery, and I meditate on the song "Mary, Did You Know?" This song always brings me to tears. Thinking of Joseph, the silent warrior, saying yes, and that simple word by both, changing the world. When life is sweet, I say, "thank you and celebrate," as Shauna Niequist has said.

Bittersweet, both pleasant and painful. It was at this time of year, in 1981, that I lost our baby in my 12th week of pregnancy. Then, two weeks later, my twenty-five-year-old husband was involved in an accident, and he died, entirely too young. But I am blessed with our beautiful daughter, who was only eighteen months old at the time, and together, we would learn to say yes to life and would survive the many challenges to come. Yes, even through tears and suffering for years, I have learned to say thank you, even when life is bitter, in order to grow. Much love and many prayers have been given to me, and I have discovered that something is always working for my good, even when I can't see it.

What I've discovered about bittersweet is this: In all things there is both something broken and something beautiful; there is a sliver of lightness on even the darkest of nights. There's a shadow of hope in every heartbreak, and rejoicing is no less rich when it contains a splinter of sadness. Sweet is so nice, but bitterness can be beautiful, full of depth and complexity, it can be courageous, gutsy, audacious, earthy.

We talk a lot about "change." Change is good in the way childbirth is good, heartbreak is good and failure also, good. I have learned the hard way that change is one of God's greatest gifts. Change is a function of God's graciousness, not life's cruelty.

I would say that, in my life, the sweet outshines the bitter. But the bitter is what has made me who I am: a compassionate, strong, loving, praying child of God.

—Denise Broussard

For your day: *When life is bittersweet, what kind of person will you choose to become?*

Day 100

I won't apologize for my tears anymore!

You need to be strong, don't cry
So I will not shed tears
Only weak people cry, don't cry
So I will not shed tears
Hurting, don't let them know, don't cry
So I will not shed tears
You grieve too deeply, don't cry
So I will not shed tears
The voices inside me and around me give such advice.

My chest aches with tears pent up!
The ache is too strong, so overwhelming!
Sliding down the front of the clothes dryer
I sit on the floor of the laundry room,
Surrounded by ozone smell and warmth.
I sit in the dark.
The dam in my heart bursts, a heave, a sob, I cry.
Only in hidden corners do I give myself permission to shed tears.

Tears become my prayers.
They are my offering to be caught up and held dear.
They are my healing balm,
An anointing for my sorrow and pain.

—Trudy Gomez

For your day: *When was the last time you allowed yourself the gift of healing tears?*

Day 101

The Revolving Door of Grief

As one stumbles and fumbles her way through the painful cycle of grief, I must constantly remind myself that there is beauty in the duality of life, and that adversity can bring some of life's greatest gifts. But it is in the painful neutral zone that these gifts must be ferreted out. In and out we go, through the revolving door of grief.

Loss illuminates the obvious and creates a stark backdrop for *Every. Single. Thing.* The Heart does not discriminate; it does not function in alignment with our mental body. It does as it pleases, opening without or against our will sometimes, and often turning the love dial much further than we are comfortable with. All completely out of our control—no pause button, no "reverse" or "rewind," no "erase." All indelible imprints that this love has etched into our soul once our loved one has passed into another dimension and into the Light of God's radiant love.

Some illuminations from the painful trough:

Ultra- sensitivity beckons one into the beautiful symphony of emotion others may never experience. The trough of the shadow side must be endured to be a worthy recipient of this gift.

The cracks and breaks in the heart are a physical sensation resembling a damaging malady of some kind. Like some cruel and instinctive voodoo that must have been cast on me by lower life forms.

Life is painfully poignant and vivid in loss. And in the next moment can feel as if cotton wool has been placed over your heart and senses, muting them while God takes over and recalibrates, cleanses, and recharges us.

There is such acute clarity in loss—flashes of memories that may have only taken seconds—but you now realize they were significant in some way to your heart, for your heart and mind have stored them.

This revolving door of emotions is what makes the human journey painfully rich and eventually rewarding.

—Ann Kergan

For your day: *JUST. HANG. ON.*

Day 102

A time to weep, and a time to laugh; a time to mourn and a time to dance.
—*Ecclesiastes 3:4*

The Gift in Tears

There are many reasons and meanings for tears. According to Merriam-Webster, they clean and lubricate our eyes in response to an irritation. A clear salty liquid spilling from our eyes and wetting our cheeks is especially an expression of emotion, whether tears of joy or tears of sorrow.

Tears of sorrow can express our heart-wrenching pain over loss: loss of trust, loved ones, marriage, children, health, virginity, dreams, and so many other things. Every Good Friday I watch the movie *The Passion* and weep as I watch Jesus suffer before and during the crucifixion. I weep as I watch Mary, His mother, so helpless, not able to stop His suffering.

When my first husband died, I cried into my pillow constantly, never wanting to reveal my vulnerability. I thought I needed to stay strong for my daughter and others. Most people want you to return to normal as quickly as possible. One day my two-year-old was crying and I was hugging her, telling her everything was going to be alright and it was ok to cry. She looked straight into my eyes and said, "No it's not, you don't cry." Wow! I thought I was doing the right thing, protecting her, when in a sense, she was saying, "I need you to really share in this sorrow with me. We are in this together." I am sharing this story because tears are truly a gift of grace, and I encourage you to share tears when appropriate.

Tears are not a sign of weakness but of strength. Jesus, David, Simon Peter, and Mary all wept. There is power in tears, soothing the pain and our sadness. They release our suffering, cleansing us, and this is the reason we just feel better after a good cry.

I'm not sure if any of you experience this, but I often laugh when I'm nervous or when I'm confronted with a difficult situation. I even cope at times of extreme sadness by smiling or laughing, which leads people who don't know me to think I don't care. I've learned that this is just my response, the way I express or control my emotions, and it's ok.

The absolute best experience is to have tears of joy and laughter. When you're with your friends, they can make you laugh till you cry. It happens at birthday parties and other celebrations. When you laugh till you are literally crying, your jaw and tummy hurt. It is so healing. Don't you just love those tears and making memories with loved ones?

Tears come with gratitude over the amazing gifts from God that come our way when we become aware to see and notice them. Tears come when you celebrate a marriage, childbirth, graduations, surviving illness or surgery. Yes, indeed, there are many gifts in tears, drawing us closer to one another, whether in sorrow or joy. That clear salty fluid that spills from our eyes to our cheeks are sacraments of love.
—Denise Broussard

For your day: *Do you allow yourself the gift of tears from joy, sorrow, and gratitude?*

Day 103

*Shiva is a Jewish term for mourning. At different stages of life,
we go through transitions and deal with what life throws at us:
getting married, leaving a marriage, taking a job, leaving a job,
having children, children leaving the nest, a family member dying,
aging, taking care of aging parents, health issue. Some things are
good, others hard, but sometimes we have to grieve those changes.
I am coming to terms with my mortality and the mortality of my
husband and being the one responsible for my 81-year-old mother.
I wrote the following as a kind of purgation. It was inspired by
circumstance and something I read in When the Heart Waits by
Sue Monk Kidd*

Sitting Shiva

I am waiting
Sitting low
Sitting Shiva
Wailing like a paid mourner
Wearing sackcloth and ashes
Tears stain my being
Grieving this transition
This change in life

I am waiting
Waiting to bury this thing I am dying to
I draw others into this funerary space
I do not want to grieve alone
It is not pity I seek or even understanding
It is companionship
Solace

I keep singing this mourning song
This dirge
Am I just regurgitating feeling, words.
Why can't I bury this
Heap on the dirt
Engrave the stone:

"Here lies this part of my life.
Gone, not forgotten
Waiting for transfiguration
And resurrection to occur,
When light and joy are reborn."

—Trudy Gomez

For your day: *What are you dying to? What life transition are you going through, grieving? Can you sit with the feelings? Can you hold the tension during the transition? Can you wait in hope?*

Day 104

Times to Mourn: Notes from My Life

Day 105

A Sensuous Life

Day 106

Saturday Mornings

Lying in bed, I listened as the house came alive.
Just as Coco awoke from her long nap,
stretching and shaking from head to toe,
so too, my house woke up.

Door bell clanging . . . .screen doors slamming.
Coffee brewing . . .laughter . . . .conversation . . .
familiar voices . . ..unfamiliar voices.
Telephone ringing . . ..washing machine spinning.
Dogs barking . . ..cats scratching
the back screen door
as the John Deere humming
wakes me up.

Empty cups at the kitchen table,
vanilla wafers and coffee
for me.
Just another Saturday morning:
cornbread in the oven
as Mama *"put on"* her soup.

The sound of gravel
dust cloud billowing.
no bell—the squeak of the screen door.
No need to look—we knew who it was.
Another Saturday morning.
Not only was it "soup day,"
it was also the day Mama fixed Aunt Helen's hair.

Rollers and pins in a Prince Albert box
weathered hands stroking her hair
under the warm water of the kitchen sink.
A bottle of color, comb and clear gloves from the medicine cabinet.
They laughed, they shared,
they sometimes complained

as the comb gently glided through the graying hair.
They consoled, they advised, they speculated
and they laughed some more as the gray disappeared.
Slowly rollers filled the hair,
bobbie pins moving from hand to hand.
Their ritual was not unlike two dancers
who knew so well,
who would lead
and who would follow.
Rollers finally in: their dance was complete.

Washing machine shaking
my insides til I'm sick.
My job: to sit
my *plan:* to listen.
Oven door opening
cornbread steaming
soup being served
with "light" bread and milk.

Like cobwebs obscuring my view,
time and space alter all memories—
all but a few.

—Jane DeBlieux

For your day*: What memories awaken your senses and emotions?*

Day 107

Things cannot be long hidden: The Sun, the Moon, and the Truth.
—Buddha

Tetrad

It was the final of four lunar eclipses:
The Blood Moon.
The lake as smooth as glass.
We sat in silence.
Each lost in thought.
The day just ending and evening just breaking.
A ribbon of red,
the last remnant of sunset weaving loosely through the mountaintops
to our backs.
The full Harvest Moon peeking over the mountaintops in front of us,
where in time the ribbon of sunset would disperse its beauty across
the barren rocks of its face.
Companions on the journey
stuck in the middle of God's majestic creation.
Inhabitants on earth
who at that moment were reminded of how minuscule we are.
We were entranced, watching the earth's shadow, our shadows
reflected off the lake's surface to the moon.
We actually saw the earth spinning as it does every second of the day
without our acknowledgement.
As our unanchored boat drifted listlessly, we saw ourselves as
spinning freely in space, precisely between the sun and the moon.
As the Moon moved completely behind Mother Earth's shadow,
we stayed connected to all those we knew.
Knowing that they were visible yet hidden in the shadow with us.
In that one moment, we were all a shadow in time, united visibly on
the surface of the moon.

—Patty Prather

For your day: *Gaze at the moon and feel yourself riding the earth*
that spins.

166

Day 108

Surprise

I love daffodils and for years have planted them on our property. Alas, South Louisiana is a bit too warm and wet for the flourishing of daffodils.

However, this morning I was on my patio when a little daffodil head bobbed up from among the ginger plants to say hello. Almost white, it was perfect in shape, and, most of all, it was a happy surprise. I felt the kiss of God for just a moment after my eyes focused and I understood what I was seeing.

It is one daffodil, but it is enough. It calls me to see the beauty of a hundred daffodils on a green hill, ruffled by the breezes. It fills me.

Pain and disappointment often come unsuspected into our lives and can leave us feeling confused and aching for a while. At these times, it is good to remember that joy can enter as a surprise as well, and nature often brings those joyful feelings wrapped in new life.

Author Christine Valters Paintner quotes poet William Stafford in her book, *Water, Wind, Earth, and Fire.* He says, "The earth we are riding keeps trying to tell us something with its continuous scripture of leaves."

I heard the voice of Spirit in my garden this morning, telling me this: "Life springs anew. Peace be still."

—Lyn Holley Doucet

For Your Day: *I will be open to surprises of joy.*

Day 109

Our morning prayers are lifted like incense on the smoke of his Cuban cigar.
—Patty Prather

What is Incense?

We think of incense as a material that, when burned, will fragrance the air. It is also smoke given off as a lifted prayer or a purifying substance.

It so touched me that Patty identified the smoke of the old man's Cuban cigar as their incense of morning prayers being lifted. This observation gave me an appreciation of all the ways in which we might be offering incense to be lifted as prayer if we but noticed the opportunity.

My morning coffee; I hold the cup between my palms and enjoy the rich aroma that travels upward. Could this be an offered prayer? Certainly it's something for which I am grateful and an appreciation sets in with the awareness.

I make soup often, and I just use what I have that day, putting in this and that until it is bubbling and releasing the wonderful aroma of a nourishing dish for us to enjoy. I could offer that, like incense, a lifted prayer.

What about the steam created from adding hot water to the dish soap and covering the dishes with it? Will that steam be a prayer lifted? Or the fragrance of the water from my mop bucket, or from the sheets warm from the dryer?

Oh, and I slip into the bath that will be my relaxing relief, creating fragrant steam of added essential oil. Definitely a prayer released. I pick up my cup of fragrant tea and sip, the aroma lifting in peaceful prayer.

—Avis Lyons LeBlanc

For your day: *What incense might you be offering every day, if you become mindful of it?*

Day 110

Colour is the language of light; it adorns the earth with beauty.
—John O'Donohue, Divine Beauty: The Invisible Embrace

I Am Blue

In the movie *The Devil Wears Prada*, Meryl Streep's character derides a young assistant with a poignant commentary on the color blue when the assistant makes the simplistic comment, "Y' know, it's just that both those belts look exactly the same to me."

I am vivid, complex, and regal, symbolizing insight and wisdom. I am the hue of the immense sky that your sunny disposition rests on at the beginning of every day.

I am like the period of Picasso revealing sadness, withdrawal, misery, cold, despair, and seeming hopelessness.

I am the pigment ultramarine derived from Lapis lazuli stone; the costly precious natural hue artists reserve for the robes of the Virgin Mary and Christ Child.

My essence is celestial and like water. I am fluid, permeating beyond the surface of the soul.

I am the Spanish lapis flecked with gold, forming beads of prayer, calming the soul, inviting it into restfulness.

I am the deeply resonant polished Chilean lapis with speckled white milky stain forming the upper nodule of the stem of the silver chalice that cradles the mystery of the divine.

I am at once haunting and soothing for those who can bear the weight of my mood.

I am the midnight shade of a moonless sky wearing a million visible stars.

I am the canvas upon which magnificent yellow can radiate its splendor.

I am varied dyes of yarns loosely interwoven in an elegant tapestry, brimming with colorful love stories discernible to those who see with the eyes of the heart.

—Elsa Diana Mendoza

For your day: *What color(s) are you? What color(s) is missing in the kaleidoscope that is your life?*

Day 111

A Sensuous Life: Notes from My Life

Day 112

Gratitude

Photo by Jill Duhon

Day 113

I am the vine, you are the branches. She who lives in me and I in her, will produce abundantly, for apart from me you can do nothing.
—John 15:5

As I reflect on the truth that I am this body of Christ, I know that being rooted in Christ, I am one with all. Today the lesson of oneness showed up in the back yard as I watched the breeze move the leaves of a pecan tree.

Leaf on a Tree

This morning I am a leaf on this tree
feeling the breeze gently moving me.
Aware of my dependence on the rest of the tree—
branches, trunk, roots, and earth—
I give thanks for my connectedness and
dwell for a while on the power of the life in this tree.
Awakening to the reality of my safety and
nourishment in this present moment,
I trust in the Goodness that provides for all my needs.
I begin to feel the strength, the comfort, the compassion
of this Mystery that holds me in this moment.
My heart expands with gratefulness for
this moment
this life
this being
the leaf of this Tree.

—Betty Landreneau

For your day: *"Live on in me, as I do in you...." (Jn 15:4) What keeps you connected to this body? How do you nourish these connections?*

Day 114

It's easy to give in to self-pity sometimes. Nature often reminds me that all of life occurs in seasons and cycles-life and death, birth and rebirth, often ushering in new sight.

Extravagance

When I was young, I kicked my can down dusty roads,
borrowed money, and made meals from fried cornmeal.

Now that I am old, I kick my can down streets of gold,
having my fill and scraping my plate, because it's

more than I could ever eat. I know poverty and I know
abundance too. I am a sister to both luxury and lack.

I lived in both houses, and both still live in me. Like an
onion, I've peeled the layers one by one until truth

began to burn and salty tears of sight I started to cry;
until all redness had washed away and blurred lines

began to clear, until the heaving began to subside and
I *finally* embraced my life just as it was, just as it is.

When I call to mind who's shoulders I stand on, and
the lessons learned from what's been lost, I see that

all was extravagant. Nothing have I lacked.

—Wendi Romero

For your day: *May I gain new sight today.*

Day 115

When "happiness" eludes us—as, eventually, it always will—we have the invitation to examine our programmed responses and to exercise our power to choose again.
—Richard Rohr

Choose Again

I am thankful that we can *choose again*. I am grateful for the many opportunities to change my heart and change my mind so that new understanding can develop and grow within me. I change in the way I see myself and the world I inhabit with so many others who are making their own choices. I am learning to let others choose, just as I am choosing.

I often say that I have been many different people in my life, and the rest of that statement is that I am thankful for it. What if I were to stay the young woman who had a comfortable childhood and live in that childhood the rest of my life? What if I never let go of my responsibility of raising children even after I have great-grandchildren to adore, with someone else being the responsible parent? Or what if I could recognize myself only as an accountant, and retirement is my current state, who am I then?

I loved all my incarnations, and I even loved most of the time I spent in them. I am, however, very glad to choose again and again. I am grateful that I have the freedom to choose.

I require a great deal of help continuing to grow, and I want to be helpful to others on their journey, hopefully as a favorable mirror. I am eternally grateful to the elegant mentors and mirrors I have and, with their help, I might keep my compass pointing true north. According to Webster: *Finding true north is essential for accurate navigation.*

—Avis Lyons LeBlanc

For your day: *Are you allowing yourself to choose again and again? Who are your mirrors and mentors who allow you to see yourself so that you can keep correcting course?*

Day 116

Sometimes I find what I'm seeking in plain sight. Acceptance of situations beyond my control have often revealed answers to my most sought-after questions.

How The Answers Came

The same questions kept repeating themselves
over and over again. They simply would not leave.

And though I asked the universe a thousand times,
the answers I wanted never seemed to come.

Then one day I finally decided to quit asking
and start accepting my one and only life, not

the one I wanted or the one I thought I had,
but the one I was given. Now, pieces of days

gone by no longer interest me. They would no
longer fit. What I used to think of myself as

odd and different, I now see as unique and gifted.

—Wendi Romero

For your day: *May I accept my one and only life, and myself, just as I am.*

Day 117

O radiant life, worthy of praise,
Awaken and reawaken the universe.
—Hildegard of Bingen

Light on a Cloudy Morning (or An Ordinary Day)

I wake at six and go sleepily into the kitchen, pressing the button on the coffee maker and looking about. I seem to run out of steam about five in the afternoon and stop cleaning, so I take stock of dishes in the sink, newspapers to throw away and too much stuff piled on the dining room table. Later, later, I would tidy up.

Yogi, our dog, rises to greet me. He is supposed to be sleeping on his bed but has probably been on the sofa; he looks guilty. I sip coffee and gather three cans of cat food, heading out the door, picking up my little calico house kitten, Zoe, as I go. She cuddles in my arms.

The light is tremulous, the fields and trees are still misty as the cats jump on their outdoor dinner table. I have this thought, *If I couldn't do this, I would miss it.*

It's "just" an ordinary day. The sun is stirring, and I, at this moment, have the grace to know there are no ordinary days, that no day will come again. The russet horse is munching on his huge hay bale. Tiny iridescent-green tree frogs cling to my cabin windows. Yogi is trying to get into the cats' bowls as the sky turns salmon-pink. I experience life as rich and radiant, even if I can hold that feeling only for moments at a time.

Dee rises and comes to join me; we sit and sip coffee together and watch the sun make a racket with color, trying to move the clouds out of the way. The little calico jumps and lands on my lap.

If I couldn't be here, I would surely miss it. I give thanks.

—Lyn Holley Doucet

For your day: *For what do I give thanks on this ordinary day?*

Day 118

Gratitude: Notes from My Life

Day 119

Freedom

Day 120

The wind of heaven is that which blows between a horse's ears.
— Arabian Proverb

Wild Mustangs

Freedom-
A strong wind blows across the western plains
tussling the mustang's long mahogany mane.
She is the head of the herd leading the stampede to higher ground.
Evading the helicopter that hovers overhead trying to corral the mustangs,
as the cowboys on their horses spread out to surround the herd.

This image of the matriarch of the herd running,
not just for herself,
but for the herds' freedom.
The freedom to roam the grassy plains as God intended is forever etched
on my heart.
The Mustangs were born to be wild.
As they flee from the impending lassos of their capture, the sunlight
bounces off their beautiful coats of varying colors. They are free. They
are majestic.

Spirit tussles with my soul implanting the same desire that lives in the wild
mustangs' DNA.

I pray to evade the lassos that steal my freedom,
and live in harmony with our Creator and His glorious creation.

I feel the lasso knot on my neck loosen.
It falls to the ground.

I run in wild abandonment toward my God.

—Patty Prather

For your day*: What lassos tie you down and pull you away from being the
authentic human being God created you to be?*

Day 121

We hold on to so much that does not serve us: old hurts and embarrassments, old fears or new ones. Think about letting go as a skill, and practice it today. As we let go and enter the present moment, we can pray more deeply.

The Skill of Letting Go

I did not know letting go
was a skill until last year.
I wish I would have known earlier.
I wasted decades holding on.
And for what? So I could stay
entrenched, entombed, entangled
to the very thing, attitude, circumstance
I wanted to avoid.

It turns out thinking is not reality.
It's only thinking.
Only reality is real.
I found this out ten years ago.
This helped me a lot except I still
kept holding on and not letting go.
I was not skilled in identifying
my thoughts as culprits.

On top of this, thoughts themselves
are skilled in tricking us
into thinking they are real.
But they are not real.
They are merely thoughts.
But now I can let go of this too.
I have acquired more skills.

—Sidney Creaghan

For your day*: Let go.*

Day 122

Save us, Savior of the world, for by your cross and resurrection
You have set us free.
—Eucharistic acclamation

Freedom

What does it mean to be free?

Am I free now?

What are those patterns from my culture, family,
education, and religion that constrict or enlarge my freedom?

When I react to an experience in life from an 'automatic mode',

I am only as free as these boundaries allow.

If I have learned to trust in the light and life within,

I can be free to respond to the invitation to stand in alignment with
the One who gives me being.

—Betty Landreneau

For your day: *What have been the most freeing moments in your life?*
How do you nourish your freedom?

Day 123

Unless you turn and become like children . . .
—Matthew 18:3

Sometimes you have to lose your adult point of view and bring out
your inner child; hopefully it is the magical child.
Do you remember that part of you?
The one who saw wonder in everything?
The one who thought anything was possible?
The one who had no prejudices?
The one who had no preconceived notions?
The one who reveled in the magic of each day?
The one who loved unconditionally?

Seeing through the eyes of my grandson reminds me of how I have
limited my magical child. We adults can stifle the magical child in
others and ourselves! I have let being a grown-up and being what
the world regards as adult color my outlook and behavior. Such an
attitude can suck the life out of mystery and magic. I let worry about
this and that and not living in the present moment overtake just being.
How do I bring that magical child back?

—Trudy Gomez

For your day: *I will embrace my magical child.*

Day 124

When I seek to control life, rather than trusting the Spirit to lead, I encounter suffering. For birds of the air, trust is as involuntary as breathing.

Open Wide

See how the feathered ones
courageously fly against
a shrouded sky.
Free from burdens
that weigh others down,
they lift their wings
and open wide.
Climbing to heights
where most dare not go,
and free from
the fear of change,
they glide on the wind.
Trust is always risky.
Some would never land,
some would never soar.

—Wendi Romero

For your day: *As the birds of the air do, may I trust the Spirit's guidance today.*

Day 125

Freedom: Notes from My Life

Day 126

Our Divine Becoming

Photo by Ann Kergan

Day 127

When troubles or worries enter our lives, remember that there is a way to find peace and solitude in God.

Threshold to the Sacred Place

There is a place where you can go

within your very soul.

A place of quiet, peace, and love

where sparks of light burst silently,

revealing hope in the darkness,

as you are held captive, timelessly

in the arms of love.

—Velma LeBlanc Cheramie

For your day: *Allow yourself to experience God's all-enveloping love in timeless peace.*

Day 128

Fill Me

Oh God . . . Father, I know you love me.
Reveal what I daily seek
but already know deep within my core.
Do not wait for me to happen upon all that is you,
for I am blind in so many ways.

Deep within, in the place we both know so well,
your little girl waits,
yearning for your touch.
I gasp for holy breath
as this world grabs me.
Sometimes I fight
and sometimes I don't ….

Lead me
guide me
protect me.
Touch me
speak to me
whisper in my ear.
I beg you, let your breath move me.

Open my eyes and make my heart bold.
Fill me with colors that reflect you and only you,
and fashion my steps with purpose, yielding light to the dark.
Not my will, but yours,
Amen
—Jane DeBlieux

For your day: *How do you wish to fill this day?*

Day 129

How do I wait with a restless heart? I grow impatient as I recall that God's timing is not my own. How do I sit with my own anticipation of things to come?

How Do I Wait

I sit at the threshold of something new.
I sense an awakening, a hesitancy too.

Spirit of anticipation, inscribe your truth
upon my heart. Make in me a womb-

to sit with what needs more time. Grant
me the patience of waiting to receive the

fullness of what is wanting to be born.
Awaken in me a desire to navigate the

inner roads, not just the outskirts of life.
As I consider all loss as necessary in light

of the sight I might gain, turn me toward
openness. Move my heart to a sacred

compassion for self and all humanity.
And when readiness arrives, pull me into

your current of love, that I might expand
outwardly like ripples from a rock tossed

into a calm lake. In every moment, may
I trust your timing and divine indwelling-

leading me to a new unfolding, a greater
incarnation of that which I already am.

—Wendi Romero

For your day: *May I trust God's timing.*

Day 130

Perhaps home is not a place but simply an irrevocable condition.
—James Baldwin

Psalm 139, Revisited

O Love, you have searched me and you have knowledge of me, you are aware of when I sit and when I stand, when I work and when I rest.

You are in my silence and you know the words I will speak before they are said. You, Love, know the intention underneath the words.

Every waking moment and every second of my sleep you draw me into you and enclose me in your tenderness.

Desiring to embody this awareness, I sit in the realization that it is too immense to achieve, too wonderful to comprehend. St. Augustine once said
"If you understand it, it is not God."

Still I cannot escape my human response of longing to know.

And yet in the same breath, there are moments I want to flee, the desire to run from you washes over me. I want to elude your probing; my soul acknowledges your piercing gaze of Love. It seems my heart cannot hold all that Life offers. Yet there is no hiding from you. You are ubiquitous—in the symphony and the dirge, in the melody and the disharmony, in the dance and the walk, in the ordinary and the extraordinary, in the tears and the laughter.

You guide me through it all, holding me even when I am not mindful of being held. You only ask that I receive, not strive to understand, but patiently wait for the unfolding. My inmost being you formed. I am aware that I must wait and while I wait I will praise you and glorify you for creating all that I am. I am remarkably and extraordinarily made. Wonderful is everything that you bring into existence.

Love, in your tenderness, examine my soul, and if you find anything misplaced or lacking of attention, by the power of your grace, I beseech you to transform the disheveled mess so that I may live in the beauty of my life and glorify you by the journey I travel.

—Deidre Montgomery

For your day: *Give thanks that you are fearfully and wonderfully made.*

Day 131

I see only what I am capable of seeing. Only when I'm ready can I see what I've never seen before.

Slow Like Waking

Slow like the spider spinning its thread
soft as silk and strong as steel.
Slow like the fern uncoiling from the pod
frond after frond.
Slow like the snake slithering on its belly
shedding its many skins.
Slow like sand collecting in the shell
going from grit to pearl.
Slow like the growing of fingers and toes
in the mother's womb.
Slow like waking from a long deep sleep
stretching into new sight-
finally seeing what can no longer hide.

—Wendi Romero

For your day: *May I see something new today.*

Day 132

Our Divine Becoming: Notes from My Life

Day 133

The True Self

Day 134

I want to travel the roads to places of beauty and light and enlightenment.

New Roads

These past few years in the second half of life, I have been exploring, taking new roads that I never would have before: byways, off the beaten tracks, trails, paths. Some have led to great self-discovery, and some have been dead ends, and that's been okay. I have rarely been lost, just temporarily misplaced. I've been traveling roads of faith and, in the words of Richard Rohr, "Faith is a journey into darkness, into not-knowing."

The not-knowing roads have allowed me to explore different artistic and creative expressions and to display them without worry about whether they are good enough. Not-knowing has helped me say yes to new experiences, to follow uncharted territories interiorly and spiritually. I have been allowing myself to follow signposts that say, "Yes, this way to you!" the ones that say, "Come follow Me!"

I often pray: *Lord, let your Spirit guide me to the truth, the Truth of You, the truth of me. Amen.*

—Trudy Gomez

For your day: *What new roads are you exploring?*

Day 135

So often I exist on the periphery of life. Sometimes giving more attention to what's out there, and sometimes succumbing to the negative energy of an environment. How do I live from a deeper place?

Toward the Heart

To live, not from the outside-in, but from
the inside-out; to move from memories

of the mind to chambers of the heart,
I revisit my own history and see how

different the future could be. I recall
that sorrow and joy are twins, a living

reality of every heart; always juxtaposed,
never to be excluded from each other.

I search deeply for lost treasures, those
hidden in plain sight. I seek my own path,

moving away from thought, and toward
the heart. The Weaver has woven a thread

of gold in and out of the seasons of my life;
and from the beginning, the weaving has

never stopped. Life is constantly moving
and so am I, but in moments of deep

listening, the Spirit is constantly revealing
to me my true identity.

—Wendi Romero

For your day: *May I seek my true identity.*

Day 136

I am who I am in the eyes of God, nothing more, nothing less.

Who Am I?

Sometimes I have asked myself, "Who am I?" I've been so many things for so many people; I lose sight of who I truly am at times. It's funny, I have thought about it, and it's easy to say all the things I'm *not* with ease.

I'm not homeless. I'm not blind. I'm not deaf. I'm not unhealthy. I'm not uneducated. I'm not a victim anymore. I'm not without faith. I'm not perfect. I'm not without troubles. I'm not without sorrows. I'm not without compassion. I'm not without joy in my heart. I'm not without laughter in my life. I'm not unloved, and so much more.

After pondering all that I'm not, why do I continue to ask, "Who am I?" It seems pretty obvious that I'm a survivor, humbled, gifted, spirit-filled, blessed, beloved daughter of God, filled with hope, peace, gratitude, and love. And, seriously, so are all of you reading this right now.

—Denise Broussard

For your day: *Let's begin to embrace our true and whole self.*

Day 137

Somewhere Inside

So long ago,
first breath.
I pause . . . I look back.
Sadness . . . joy . . . shame
regret, hope, and awe.
What does God see when He looks at me?
Moving from no faith
to protestant
to Catholic
to what?
I see God in everything.
no borders, no restrictions,
no limits to who He is.
He loves me.
She speaks to me.
My God holds me
and mothers me home.
somewhere inside of me
is His idea
yet to be.

—Jane DeBlieux

For your day: *Who do you see when you look inside?*

Day 138

It takes intention and practice to tune out the negative voices of past conditioning. Unless I'm tuned to vibrations of love, I may never experience the truth of who I really am.

Clarity

Sometimes it takes
years of wandering
alone in the woods
before you begin
to hear the soft
babble of the brook,
the gentle rush of
the river, or the
fearless fall of water
calling from a higher
place—speaking your
name in a way
only your soul can
understand.

—Wendi Romero

For your day: *May I listen to my soul.*

Day 139

The True Self: Notes from My Life

Day 140

Random Graces

Photo by Avis Lyons

Day 141

My soul finds rest in God alone.
—Psalm 62-1

Insomnia

Insomnia has wrapped its curse around me.
The night as black as coal.

In the distance the sound of a train whistle,
the vibrations from the train gently rocking my bedroom walls.

The whistle grows fainter.
Is it the train's far off cry that I hear
or my own cry,
too far off to be heard by anyone?

The train beckons to me.
Our cries of warning drawing us together.

The insomnia loses its grip.
I am lulled to sleep with an awareness,
that in the loneliness of a dark night
God still finds a way to speak to me.

—Patty Prather

For your day: *List some different ways that God speaks to you. Are some more frequent than others? Are you open to new avenues to hear His call?*

Day 142

One day, I meditated with my friends at Sacred Center when a poem from Blue Horses, by Mary Oliver was read in which she remembered so much gloom in her childhood. I chose a word from my childhood that came to mind.

Silence

I closed my eyes and began to think about a word that might describe my childhood. The word *silence* came to me quickly and vividly. It wasn't the sacred silence I experience during meditations that make my life clearer to me. What I remembered was what is referred to as the silent treatment. This was a silence in which I did not know where I stood, or what I had done, or if one was angry with me. It made me edgy, nervous, and very uncomfortable but unable to move to get away. I never knew what to do. Should I please, should I ask what was wrong, or if I had done anything? To this day, when someone is silent with me, I feel a tight tension and nervousness throughout my body, but mostly in my heart. I feel defeated like that small child I see from my past.

Sometimes, I recall that as a teenager I visited a favorite spot shaded with massive oak trees on a high grassy area off what is known as Grosse Isle, on the family farm, far away from the silent kitchen. I'd look toward our family home and think how it would be for me as an adult. Would I marry and make a home near here? I also thought that when I was an adult, I would never feel this silence and that I would certainly not put my loved ones through this type of pressure. I hoped I would speak out with love and kindness and assurance of my love. I would not make them suffer from the silent treatment as I had, sometimes wondering if I was really loved. I wanted to assure my future family of my love for them. I often think of my spot under the oak trees, slowly swinging on a small tractor tire swing, all now non-existent, and how it did save me from a silence that formed me and encouraged me not to be this way in my life.

—Cheryl Delahoussaye

For your day: *Think of your childhood and write about the word that comes to your mind.*

Day 143

Life is continuously moving, and time does not stand still to display its precious moments. We have to stop to see it.

Hourglass

I looked at an hourglass intently one day
noticing the metaphor it truly is,
upright and secure,
a balanced visual
illustrating the present,
transforming into the past.

Tiny grains of seconds moving quickly
falling into the small hole of now,
creating time as we know it,
the sand then landing gently
building upon a heap of time passed,
adding to collected memories.

I studied the hourglass again, on a tilt.
Time moved more slowly,
trickled with less force.
I could see the grains more clearly.
I liked it that way.

After a moment of enjoying the idea
of slowing down time,
I set the hourglass back
to its upright and secure position,
turned it over,
and smiled with acceptance.

—Jill Duhon

For your day: *Praise God for all the grains of seconds that create the moments that make your day a gift.*

Day 144

If anyone cleanses himself of these things, he will be a vessel for lofty use, dedicated, beneficial to the master, ready for every good work.
—*2 Timothy 2:21*

Why Not Me?

When I was younger, I would ask, "Why me?" Trauma and tragedy started at birth and followed me into adulthood. Abandonment, sexual abuse, addictions, and I experienced my first death of a loved one when a boyfriend committed suicide when we were only 18 years old. I was the last person he spoke to that day, so I carried guilt for years. I learned, through the practice of silence, that guilt was not mine to carry.

When all these issues happened, I had no control over them. I was young and couldn't talk about them to anyone. I thought either no one would understand or no one would believe me. I couldn't share the pain, so I froze. This word "frozen" is exactly how I felt: fear, guilt, shame, mistrust, no voice, and thinking why me? I spiraled into a self-destructive journey for years with alcohol and drugs, which only numbed the pain for short periods of time.

Richard Rohr, a Franciscan priest and teacher, says, "When we cannot face and embrace the insecurities inside ourselves, we project them outwardly, hating the self we see mirrored in the "other." Another of my favorites from him: "All great spirituality is about what we do with our pain. If we do not transform our pain, we will transmit it to those around us."

I was not evil, never wanted to hurt others, only wanted to hurt myself. People hurt us, and we turn around and focus on harming ourselves. I, like my children, who have dealt with their own traumas, just labeled our actions as dumb decisions. Now I understand that self-destructive behavior is usually driven by underlying and unresolved issues. Life is such a teacher and such mystery.

The parents of the child that is on that path usually ask, "What have I done wrong? Did I not give them enough? Did I not love them enough? Did I not teach them right from wrong? Did I not go to church enough? Why are

212

they doing this to me, don't they love me?" For the parent, it becomes an "all about me" syndrome. I share now when talking to parents who don't understand their child's actions or who feel guilty, that we have no earthly idea where their life's journey has taken them. My parents certainly did not until I was an older and stronger adult.

I was talking with a friend whose son died when he was very young. She says that "why me?" was never really productive, and it also feels like wishing harm or sadness on someone else. We both have managed to handle life's stumbling blocks the best we could and with a good heart. Her words to me: "Into every life a little rain must fall, even when it comes in unrelenting waves. The good news is you reached a place where you accept challenges with grace, fueled by faith and with a wonderful grateful spirit." I know many friends for whom these words ring true.

Now that I have gotten older, with centering prayer and silence, I can and do embrace, "Why not me?"
Abandonment has been replaced with God's everlasting presence. Sexual abuse feelings of mistrust and shame have been replaced with knowing they are in good hands with our Father. Now I believe they were gifts and not my possessions to begin with.

Why not me? To be a vessel, to be used by God, to share hope, joy, laughter, and, most of all, love. God's purpose for our lives is far greater than any problem we come up against.

—Denise Broussard

For your day: *I pray that you seek what God has for you and that you become the vessel described in 2 Timothy 2:21.*

Day 145

My teacher can be anyone or anything in my life, if I am aware.
This day I noticed the vertical blinds being moved by the air from
the ceiling fan.

Vertical Blinds

Just notice: the vertical blinds
made to be identical widgets—each swaying to its own rhythm
in the breeze created by the ceiling fan.
I don't judge them as being
    superior or inferior
    right or wrong
    expensive or cheap.
I put many people or things
on an either/or scale, labeling them as one thing or another.
In the now: all I am invited to do is be present
to what is in me,
around me,
so that
what is designed to flow through me
may be unimpeded.

—Betty Landreneau

For your day: *Who/what is your teacher today?*

Day 146

Random Graces: Notes from My Life

Day 147

Our Courage and Strength

Day 148

Life Force

Toxic fumes have enveloped me.
The air is thin and my breath is labored.
I am backed into a corner, weary and alone.
The rain reflects my tears.

I feel tied to a post while barbs are thrown at me
and sarcasm cuts my skin.
Nurturing is the medicine I need,
cherishing me as a salve soothes a wound.

There exists a hole inside me, beginning to glow.
It is as necessary to me as air.
The women in my life are showing me how to
kindle the fire and keep it burning.

Labor pains, unavoidable pains, have begun.
There is a life to live and a light to be seen and felt.

—Rita B. Vincent

For your day: *What keeps my light glowing? How am I nurtured?*

Day 149

Our world is overflowing with distractions and the challenge to respond to life from my true center is constantly before me. I must be mindful to access the power of presence.

The Power of Presence

Everyday I awaken with a hungry heart
starving for true bread. With expectant

longing, I look to see how this day will be
made new again; to see how stories of an

unforgotten past might be written over
and elongated shadows reshaped. Life

happens right here, right where I stand,
and not in some foreign country I might

wander to in my mind. At every moment,
may I witness wonder, seeing what is

appearing directly in front of me. As I
travel the curving roads of life, may I be

filled with the knowing that when bends
break and turns toss, I am not lost nor

do I travel alone. Where I am weak and
and my knees buckle, may compassion

be softly whispered in my ear. May I be
carried until I am strong enough to stand,

and may the coming and going of my sight
always be guarded. But if it should fail me

and I'm no longer capable of seeing beauty,
face-to-face, may my awareness be trans-

formed so that the original seed of blessing
planted in me from eternity awakens once

more and sprouts to new life.

—Wendi Romero

For your day: *May I experience the power of mindful presence.*

Day 150

The Lord will watch over your coming and going both now and forevermore.
—Psalm 121:8

The Worlds Born of Chaos

I take great heart in Psalm 121:8 because I often wonder about whether to come or go, whether to stop or start—all the choices to be made. I know to ask for God's guidance, but I sometimes forget that I have the comfort of assistance, and so I often wrestle with the choices on my own.

Among my friends, the topic of chaos often comes up. We talk about the chaos that comes before the new form emerges. Just as the phoenix rises from the ashes to a new existence, new worlds are born out of chaos. We discuss how to know when one thing has ended and another is on the way, and how to wait in that space of no longer and not yet.

We all experience chaos when change is in its natural time as well as when change is thrust upon us. We often tolerate chaos when it is simple disorder and sometimes continue to tolerate it when we are feeling as if we are going mad before we embrace the change, move with it, and see what's next. Madness often occurs when we hold on to someone or something beyond its life expectancy. Our life becomes vulnerable to the madness when the storyline has ended, and we have to cut and paste a story from bits and pieces and shuffle them around to make it acceptable for us to hold on longer.

When I am with a friend in turmoil of decision, I often ask her to look for the joy. I think God wants us to be joyful people. Not as in happy or having fun but joyful, or at least, have the suggestion of being joyful. If a choice is not joyful, then I think it might not be the best choice. It seems to me that joy has a present-moment quality. Joyful brings you right here, right now: God's place. I would also ask which choice gives you some relief, some breathing space? Feel some small place where the chaos isn't, where a measure of relief can be felt. Relief and breathing space are also God's place, present time, presence.

Most of my life I have behaved as if my balance and health were not my responsibility. I know I believed that my thoughts were not correctible, and things happened to me. I just lived in the past, in the future, and in madness as if my being could withstand the onslaught of whatever terrible things I wanted to tell and whatever nonsense crossed my path. I now know that I am responsible to my piece of this existence, and as a responsible person of God's creation, I need to be alert to where I put my attention.

To be in my body, responsible for the way I engage life, is a constant choice and a constant hope of success. Still, there's the question of how to recognize when it's time to let go or to persevere. Is it joyful and life-affirming for all concerned? Am I putting into this energy I can ill afford, with no light at the end of the tunnel? These are the hard questions, and the chaos will go from disorder to madness if we hang on too long.

Sometimes it takes total destruction of our safe little place for us to move away from the confusion of chaos. Sometimes we move to another, but same, safe little place and must repeat the confusion and madness of chaos over and over until we discover even a tiny, new and different way on our path.

If we just remember, God is watching over our comings and goings, is always and everywhere our relief in the chaos.

—Avis Lyons LeBlanc

For your day: *In the chaos of life, find a place to breathe with God, find the relief God offers, and wait for the guidance.*

Day 151

Unraveling

Fear
a shadow that follows its prey.
Why are we so afraid?
Be courageous, they say.
Face your fears, they say.
Be you, they say.

Like it or not, deep within we know
the unraveling when it begins.
Anxiously we seek the cleansing,
the break, the opening, the first full breath
but at what cost?

Come in, Fear, have a seat
make yourself at home.
Why do we usher in what we know
binds us to darkness?

No one wants to be vulnerable, exposed, or naked.
That might invite what we fear most: rejection.
Why do we hide who we are
from the God who dwells in our fellow man?

God knew rejection, exposure, vulnerability,
brokenness, ridicule, and humiliation.
He knows our fear.
He quietly waits for us
to come to him, and yet
we still hide.

My God, my Father,
my Brother, my Friend,
never tire of loving me – I need you.

When you see me run,
when you see me hide
pull me close.

Breathe your Spirit into me,
whisper in my ear and dispel my fear.

Like delicate hands
working deliberately, yet gently,
to pull apart a twisted knot,
may Your love reveal a NEW me,
the REAL me that you know and love.

Sustain me, my God, my Protector,
as I learn each day to love and accept
the cracks that make me who
I am.

—Jane DeBlieux

For your day: *Have you begun to unravel? Ask God to gently pull apart your twisted parts to set free the real you.*

Day 152

Happiness is not a matter of intensity, but of balance, and order, and rhythm, and harmony.
—Thomas Merton

YOLO Board

A Yolo board is a standup paddle board that offers fun and a full body workout, but also a relaxing way to play on the water. Yolo is an acronym for "you only live once". I love the saying and I absolutely loved the ride. I wasn't sure if I would be capable of standing up on the Yolo board, but I was not leaving the beach without trying. What a gift it was, in so many different ways, and I want to share my thoughts about the experience.

My family told me that a person needed core strength and balance to ride. I found this to be true immediately and fortunately my daughter called me an "instant Yolo pro." The physical gifts of the ride were obvious; sounds of water splashing against the front of the board as I glided with ease, watching schools of fish swimming under the water, and seeing pelicans flying overhead looking for their next meal. The gentle breeze kept me cool on a hot day, and I embraced the beauty of the clear water and blue sky. The best part for me was the stillness way out in the deep. The serenity was magical and a little scary if I thought too much of what could be swimming under me. I was excited and proud to step out of my comfort zone and be a bit daring. This added to my pleasure. (I must not forget, I wore a life jacket for physical survival, because I was out so far from shore.)

As I'm riding I begin to have a conversation with my Holy One. The One who has made all of this to enjoy and He wants us to enjoy to the fullest. My son was in a kayak nearby and I shared these ideas with him, and He told me he was experiencing the same thing. (He said he thinks he might have been a fish in another life, because he can't stay out of the water.)

My spiritual experience riding on the board gave me thoughts of life, rhythm, and balance. I speak a lot of joy and sorrow, because from an early age I experienced it all. Life is all about balance with the good and the bad, highs and lows, laughter and tears, the stressful and the peaceful times. I trust that my Holy One is and has been my life jacket ensuring my soul's survival. My family told me I needed core strength and balance, which I believe I receive through my Heavenly Father. I want to embrace life, love unconditionally and always trust that my Father in heaven loves me. Yes, we only live once, so let's live life to the fullest.

—Denise Broussard

For your day: *What do we need and what do we love, in order to balance the body and soul?*

Day 153

Our Courage and Strength: Notes from My Life

Day 154

Self and Union

Photo by Patty Prather

Day 155

Getting caught up in my day-to-day routine, it's easy to forget who I really am. I often need to be reminded.

Meeting Place

I am a meeting place,
an intersection of
nature and spirit—
to be filled,
emptied,
and filled again.
I am the presence
of a far deeper reality.
I possess an undeniable
strength, and at my weak
places, I am made strong.
I am a vessel of life,
filled with hope,
filled with light.

—Wendi Romero

For your day: *May I remember who I truly am.*

Day 156

Sometimes there are just no words to adequately describe the present, like deep love, gratitude, a place in nature—even beyond awe.

Beyond the Word

Beyond the word,
without a language,
toward the eternal,
across the line of reason,
through the clouds of ambiguity
in the presence of the divine . . .

There is a space, a realm,
that transcends understanding,
that surpasses human limitations.

On God's timeless vertical,
we receive His gift.
Beyond the word,
without a language
is . . .

—Jill Duhon

For your day: *Our actions can often describe our feelings, without having to put words to them. A tight hug with a sincere smile says so much. Experience loving those you meet today beyond words.*

Day 157

We can help co-create an energetic field of peace as we choose peace within our own hearts.
—Global Coherence Initiative

We Are All One

I am a thread in the wholeness of life.
A fiber, vibrating toward and from
this web of oneness.
This field of all
pulses our world,
revealing who we are.
Loving and compassionate.
Resentful and complaining.
The field responds: no judgment.
I pray for awareness,
for self-regulation,
watching my actions,
hearing my words,
feeling my emotions,
listening to my thoughts.
For I can choose to be
the change I want to see.
I can choose to be
a thread of compassion
in the field where all is one.

—Avis Lyons LeBlanc

For your day: At the end of the day, perhaps "the Examen" as Ignatius of Loyola recommends would be of great benefit. This is a version of the five-step Daily Examen that St. Ignatius practiced.

- *Become aware of God's presence.*
- *Review the day with gratitude.*
- *Pay attention to your emotions.*
- *Choose one feature of the day and pray from it.*
- *Look toward tomorrow.*

Day 158

I can live life only a moment at a time. So much can be realized in a single moment.

No Other

Only to this moment do I belong.
It contains the whole world.
There is no other canvas to be painted,
no other story to be told,
no other song to be sung.

Only to this moment do I belong.
I must trust it with every cell of my being,
like salt in water, dissolving completely
into the place where your breath is mine
and my heart beats in your heart, too.

Only to this moment do I belong.
There is no other. I must keep
a close watch with you or I'll continue
to stumble in the dark, bumping into
what I have yet to see.

—Wendi Romero

For your day: *May I be truly present, one moment at a time.*

Day 159

Words are the Ignition Point of your Manifestation

Words hold power,
And Energy
We have not been raised by our Elders
To Honor this power.
We are the New World.
The Conscious Ones.
We must push through and live the Truth.
Of who we are.
Spirit in Human Form.

Know that we create our own world
Through our thoughts
And our words.
Choose them wisely.
Guard them like precious cargo.

Test it and see
Speak your wishes, desires and dreams
And watch them manifest.
Feel your dreams becoming reality.
As if it has already happened.
Because it is through the *FEELING* nature
That worlds are created
And our dreams manifest.
Namaste

—Ann Kergan

For your day: *May I choose my words carefully.*

Day 160

Self and Union: Notes from My Life

Day 161

A Life of Transformations

Day 162

At Pope Francis's request, the annual observance on the Catholic calendar of St. Mary Magdalene has been made a major feast, marking women as the first evangelizers.
—Press Release from Rome concerning an official letter issued by the Vatican's Congregation for Divine Worship.

Lead Our Hearts to the Good

I am a Mary Magdalene champion. I am distressed that she was ever portrayed as a prostitute when there is no biblical evidence that she was. I also am sad that she never took her place (in the collective consciousness) as a virtuous and devoted disciple and leader of the early church. It seems that passing centuries and certain political forces buried her legacy. However, she seems to be rising out of time and speaking to us once again of her primary importance to Christ. British Archbishop Arthur Roche says, "In fact, between the times she encountered Christ at the tomb and when she proclaimed the resurrection to them (male disciples) *Mary Magdalene was the church on earth because only she understood the full meaning of Jesus's ministry.* (Italics mine.)

What can all of this mean to us women who seek to follow Christ? So often, the Blessed Mother, Mary, has been the main womanly example for us all to follow, and indeed, she is still so important. And thank God for her. But, on the other hand, it would be difficult for us to relate to Jesus as his mother. More comfortably, we can be in relationship with him as Mary Magdalene was: he is our mentor, brother of spirit, teacher, and Lord.

Mary Magdalene, as we know, encountered Jesus resurrected in the garden. At first thinking him to be the gardener, she asks him to show her the body of the Lord. Then Jesus says her name, "Mary!" and she recognizes him. Her response is interesting, "Rabboni!" She is saying, "Teacher!"

We can embrace Jesus as teacher, not of facts but of a way of life. This is the way of life that lets the last be first, feeds the hungry, embraces peace. We seek to remove the boulder from our own eyes before we criticize another. We struggle with being kind. We open ourselves to love. On our good days, we even consider the lilies of the fields and our place in the cosmos, our lives and our deaths and the ultimate meaning of it all.

Among the French devotees of Mary Magdalene, this line is often heard, "She leads our hearts to the good." I invite us to ponder that this morning, for a just bit. May this other Mary lift up our hearts.

—Lyn Holley Doucet

For your day: *How might Mary Magdalene lead your heart to the good?*

Day 163

It is so important to live the questions, to live them into the present moment. After you read this reflection, consider what questions your heart is asking. What is opening for you now?

And Now What?

And now what? The questions keep appearing, but they do not hold my attention in the same way as before.
Before what? Before the time had come.
What time? The time Love gave me to discover.
Discover what? Discover the true essence of me.
Where was she? She was hidden under all that I *thought* was me.
Who was that? A fear-based, insecure illusion of a beautiful woman who thought she was in control.
In control of what? In control of life.
Now what? Now she seeks to allow Life.
"Isn't that passive?" Ego asks.
No. Allowing requires participation through non-resistance, which means saying, YES to whatever Life offers.
What does Life offer? Breath in this moment.

"Every soul that uplifts itself uplifts the world"—Elisabeth Leseur (1866-1914)

My deepest desire is to desire Love's will. When my capacity to love grows, I can, through grace, *live in the allowing* more often. The anxiety, fears, disappointments, and frustrations do not last as long, and the peace, joy, contentment, and excitement are recognized with more ease.

My prayer is to turn myself over completely to Love—without condition, without reserve—*to allow.* My prayer is to no longer want anything or fear anything. My prayer is to desire nothing but what Love desires.

—Deidre Montgomery

For your day: *I ask the questions, I live in not knowing. I rejoice in love's choice.*

Day 164

Sometimes my resistance to change causes me much turmoil. Then I remember that change is seasonal and there's no way around it. Life is change.

Turning Toward

Like the seasons, I am turning.
All of life is a turning—turning
toward what is and away from
what is not. At intersections
I wait, at odd angles I stand.
A velvet hammer strikes the gong
of my soul, shattering illusions
that this will always be.
Beggar I become, praying what
I want to stay and away what I don't.
But like the river, the current pulls
and the winds change. In my turning,
what to do with dead leaves
and dried bones that have washed
up on my shore, but bow to them—
turning toward, no longer stalling
but squaring off face-to-face with
what is. The river curves, every drop
in search of the sea. Fiery flame of
burning love, be my lighthouse.
Steer me clear at every turn.

—Wendi Romero

For your day: *May I turn toward life today.*

Day 165

Transformation

While browsing through past journals recently, I was pleased to find evidence of the way God guided me over a period of three years. It wasn't a surprise because I know he is ever present in my life but even so, it is amazingly delightful to me.

Journal Date September 30, 2003
For a long time now – since Moma died (April 2001) – I have had a sense that the old 'me' is fading away. Velma, the long-awaited daughter of Annie, that little girl who made her mother so happy. The girl who was nice, ladylike and dutiful to make everyone around her happy, that Velma is waning. She is evolving to become my "Father's daughter", the person God intended her to be.

I know, Lord, you have a plan for me, for I am still here on this earth to become the daughter you would have me be. I really feel it inside. Permission to be ME granted - permission to love as I felt loved today. Two little arms wrapped around my neck, heartbeat to heartbeat while we "swinged" on our back-porch swing – singing our very own little song - swing, swing, swing, swing … weeee, weeee; swing, swing, swing, swing …weeee, weeee!

My grandkids love it! I love it!

They love me! I love them!

Your love shared! Swing, swing, swing, swing … weeee weeee!

Just as God called Jacob to become Israel and Peter to become Cephas, I feel myself being called to become Anne. It is so fitting that I become Anne in the fall, my favorite season of the year with its autumn leaves, cool soft breezes and all of my favorite colors. Over my mantel hangs a beautiful picture called September. Yes. It is time for acceptance of what is and what is to come.

I believe. I receive. I thank you Lord. You are in my heart. Lead me on to become, observe, and receive the gifts you send to me through every person in my life. I receive all as opportunities for you to reveal yourself to me, Anne, your new creation. Make me a channel, Lord, that others may see you through me. This is my prayer and I thank you Father.

"So whoever is in Christ is a new creation: the old things have passed away; behold, new things have come." 2 Corinthians 5:17

Love, Anne

Journal Date August 23, 2004

I am a Louisiana Iris (wildflower) and my name is Anne. Lavender petals turning to deep purple in its center with hues of pinks, blues and a white-hot spark of flame burning deep in its throat, refusing to fade or die – this flame is what sustains me though it is hardly visible.

When I pictured myself as a wildflower, I seemed wilted and weak. I asked God to show me why my heart is so divided. He said that I did not face Him to receive His love because I feel undeserving.

God said, "I do not love you because you deserve my love. I love you because I am love ... and love loves. You must lift your head up high to receive my love that you may grow in beauty and in strength."

Father/Mother God, I will bend in the breezes and search the heavens for your face that you may be glorified by the changes in me.

Jesus, I trust in you to help me bend until I get myself upright. Amen.

Journal Date December 24, 2005

"My name is not Velma; Velma is my address." This was told to me by my soul on this day.

Up until now, I have never honored my new name by telling anyone about these little gifts from God.

I have always been too timid and fearful. My full birth name is Velma Ann LeBlanc with my married name Cheramie. God added one little letter to my middle name giving honor to St. Anne who has always held a special place in my heart being that I, too, am a grandmother. I am a new creation in Christ; I am now called Anne.

—Velma LeBlanc Cheramie

For your day: *Journaling has helped me get through some very difficult times and it has proved rewarding to look back to see the progress God makes in me. If you were to journal today, what would you journal? A simple prayer each day is a good beginning.*

Day 166

God continues to whisper, in that still small voice, "When are you truly gonna trust me?"

Prayer is our Connection

Early one morning as I rode my bike, I was listening to the song, "The Prayer" by Celine Dion and Andrea Bocelli. It brought back happy memories of my son and me riding in the car, listening and singing the song together. I would sing Celine's part and he would sing Andrea's. My prayer that particular morning went like this, "Son, wherever you are, whatever you are doing, hear this song, please feel this song in your heart right now. Know you are never alone." And "Lord keep nudging us, don't let us go, and make us aware of your presence."

Later that same day, I was at Crossroads book store, purchasing gifts, and I bought him and myself an Immaculee "three time blessed" bracelet with St. Benedict medals. These medals are used to ward off spiritual and physical dangers, especially related to temptations. The moment I left to get in my car, my cell phone rang. It was a text from my son. It read, "Lead us to a place, guide us with your grace, give us faith so we'll be safe :) I love you mom, just listened to that song. I love you and dad so much." These are the lyrics to the song, "The Prayer" I prayed with that same morning.

I sat in my car, weeping with some disbelief but mostly joy and gratitude, for God not letting us go and helping us to be aware of His presence and love. I responded to the text immediately, telling him about my morning bike ride, the song and my prayer for him. His text left no doubt that the Holy Spirit is moving, and we are so connected. My friend asked me when I shared this God experience, "Denise, what more do you want? Writing in the sky?"

—Denise Broussard

For your day: *Are there places where you need to trust God enough to let things happen without striving to predict or control them?*

Day 167

A Life of Transformations: Notes from My Life

Day 168

Be Tender with Yourself

Photo by Deidre Montgomery

Day 169

But Jesus often withdrew to the wilderness and prayed.
—Luke 5:16

Being Still

I am missing my centering prayer group this morning, tying up loose ends, to go on a silent retreat in Grand Coteau at the Jesuit Spirituality Center. Yes, I am being drawn into silence and heading to the wilderness. I used to be satisfied if I experienced one trip of solitude in a year, but now I seem to be desiring this more and more. I say yes to solitude because this brings me great peace and healing. When friends and family ask me, "What are you going to do?" I smile, with no guilt, and say, "Absolutely nothing, just spend time with God and His creation."

Solitude to me is being alone with God, drawing closer to Him. Just to be with his creation and enjoy the moon and stars, sunsets, sunrises, beautiful oak trees, birds, the breeze, and yes, even the rain. When the rain comes, I'm certain I will shed some tears. Part of my sorrow comes from considering the many who are suffering, or it comes from remembering pain in my own past. But some of my tears come because I am so grateful for the many blessings God has bestowed upon me. I'm still working on "letting go" and "surrendering all" because, as I've said a million times, I am a work in progress.

As I pray for my sacred sisters, I trust they will also be praying for me and my family, that they all stay safe and healthy while I'm away.

I will certainly retreat, relax, renew, replenish.

It's what the Great Physician has ordered. If nothing else, I will get much needed rest.

—Denise Broussard

For your day: *Can you spend time with God and His creation today? Where might you find a wilderness place for peace and healing?*

Day 170

Do not live in the shadow of the masters forever. Learn to live in the light of your soul. Life deserves full expression.
—*Amit Ray*

My Shadow

My shadow casts shade over patches of the dry earth.
My soul has loosed the bonds of my blood and bones and falls before me.
It pours the gray/black color of my shadow into the tiniest of cracks in the sidewalk.

My shadow gives the gift of restful shade to the smallest of insects, on this hot summer day. This small crack filled with dark soil is home to the smallest of creatures who spend their day exploring the wealth of unseen miracles within their countries borders. The insects are just as busy with their jobs and survival as we humans.

Depending on the angle of the sun my shadow crosses those whose faces are invisible to me, because they walk behind me. Yet we are physically united by my shadow and we are one. I say a prayer of thanksgiving for their lives and for the gift of the sun. I turn the corner, the sun at my back.

Once again my shadow is cast forward offering shade to humans and four legged creatures as they approach.

I become aware of the red tail hawk winging above us casting his protective shadow of shade over us, and I am drawn spiritually into the depths of the sea. I see a Great Blue whale with the sun bouncing off her back as she breaks the surface for a life giving breath, her tremendous shadow touching all the life below her in the darkest depths of the sea as she devours a portion of her daily meal. I am humbled by the vision.

—Patty Prather

For your day: *When you see your shadow pay attention to what it may be calling you to attend to in your spiritual life. Or just take time to revel in seeing you projected as a blank slate. No wrinkles, no warts, only you.*

Day 171

What no eye has seen, what no ear has heard and what no human mind has conceived, are the things God has prepared for those who love him.
—1 Corinthians 2:9

Divine Surprises

My first retreat for this year was full of surprises and my heart was open for whatever God prompted me to do. I had signed up for a yoga and contemplative prayer retreat. I have been enjoying and practicing silence and contemplative prayer for several years, but doing yoga would be stepping out of my box. My Lord had many surprises in store for me, and I have become aware that He does that all the time, when I listen and say yes.

I arrived with my yoga mat and couldn't wait for the stretching, praying, and breathing. I looked at yoga as just another avenue of prayer. I considered yoga as union with God, and Jesus would be my yoga teacher. Then I heard that drumming and art would be included. So I thought, "What? Seriously?" I don't do either of those things, but my heart was open.

I immediately felt comfortable with the Djembe drum. Drumming is like the rhythm of life. We need rhythm in our busy lives, with our responsibilities pulling us in so many different directions. I need rhythm, being drawn to more silence to deepen my connection with my Lord and with others. I thought about how Jesus had rhythm, regularly withdrawing from life, the crowds, and going into the wilderness to have quiet time with His Father. This rhythm gave him the ability to enter such rich relationships with others while he carried out his mission. He gave hope, wisdom, and love. (He is my idol and I want to be just like Him when I "grow up.") Because I have always been a lover of all types of music, I realized that, for me, it creates order out of chaos. I also learned that a good drummer "listens" as much as he or she plays. I truly enjoyed this divine surprise.

Another surprise presented to me was "collaging." I discovered I could be creative all by myself with no one having to instruct me. I enjoyed looking in magazines, spotting pictures and words that just popped out for me. Then it was fun to cut, glue, and create my own piece of art. My finished work of the day ended up speaking of love in many ways.

During our art session, a ladybug landed on me. I didn't think anything of it, but the next day when the retreat was over, I was in Jennings, and it happened again. I googled the meaning of ladybug and this led to another surprise. (I do believe the ladybug is my new friend.) This is what I read on the computer: "The old weight and habit of debt is lifted from you and your life. The appearance heralds a time in which wishes will be fulfilled, worries begin to dissipate and new happiness comes about. Let things flow at their natural pace, not trying too hard or going too fast." And this last phrase really spoke to my spirit, "Do not be scared to live your truth, protect your truth and know it's yours to honor." Ladybug

I'm in a good place, with so much more love, wisdom, and hope to give to others. I'm grateful that I am aware of His divine surprises.
—Denise Broussard

For your day: *Can we open our hearts, listen, and see the surprises with which God blesses us each day?*

Day 172

Above all, trust in the slow work of God.
—Pierre Teilhard DeChardin

Expectations and Anticipation

I realize that in my first half of life, I lived with a lot of expectations and in anticipation. This is not a bad thing, but it can leave us with huge disappointments or feelings of failure. When things don't go as we planned or in the time frame we want, we're devastated. It has taken me many years to realize, "I am not in control."

As young women, we try so hard to meet the expectations of others. Whether it's from parents, friends, family, or co-workers, any outside validation, no matter how frequent, is never enough. We literally try our hardest to raise perfect children in an imperfect world. We speak of how good we are at "multi-tasking" to the point of burn-out, because we think that is what is expected of us.

With my own life and the lives of my children, family, and friends, I believed I could and did know what was best for myself and for other people. Then, because I thought I knew best, I had no problem sharing my important information and suggestions with anyone who would listen. I thought that, surely, if I just did enough, I could control my body and the lives of those around me. I'm finally learning to let go of expectations for myself and for others. I trust in God's timing, not mine.

My wise daughter has asked me many times, when she hears frustration in my voice, "Mom did they ask you for your advice?" I have to humble myself and answer truthfully, "No." I've come to realize that others just need me to listen. An Irish proverb tells us, "God gave us two ears and one mouth, so we ought to listen twice as much as we speak."

In my second half of life, with much prayer, with silent retreats, and my centering-prayer group, I am working on stepping out of "expecting and anticipating." I am learning to accept that each person has his/her own life and has every right to the journey. I have to move out of God's way so He can do what's best for each individual. I don't think my way is the best way anymore.

For me, it's about letting go, living one day at a time, showing compassion, and as I say a lot, "It is what it is. And it all belongs." I am so grateful to my Heavenly Father that I've lived long enough to embrace this second half of life. I understand how life is brief, how life is full of mystery, and how much He loves me. I say goodbye to expectations and anticipations, trusting Him, which takes the burden off me.

—Denise Broussard

For your day: *Can we trust and be thankful that He will meet all our needs?*

Day 173

From the beginning, the untouched radiance of the Divine dwells within. There is nothing we need to do to earn it. It is our birthright. It already is.

I Am Enough

There is nowhere else I need to be
except the very place I am.

There is nothing else I need to do
except be present right where I stand.

Each slice in time, a mystical encounter
with the Divine. This is my compass-

it's how I know I'm not lost. I won't rush
this meeting place of life, yours across mine.

I can't hurry the healing of my sacred
wounds, I can only die to the reasons why.

There is no right or wrong way to go, only to
travel lightly with nothing unnecessary in tow.

Anything extra would be too much.
Just as I am is more than enough.

—Wendi Romero

For your day: *May I always know that I am enough.*

Day 174

Be Tender with Yourself: Notes from My Life

Day 175

Mystical Glimpses

Day 176

Manna from Heaven

You are invited to experience paradise
along with a cup of coffee at sunrise.

A festive, magical atmosphere dominates the landscape.

There are poetry groups spread out for miles around
and beyond the lake.

We are all there for the annual exchange of words.

I was mesmerized by the hundreds of barrels of
red apples,
each with a different word group inscribed on its skin.

In addition, there are wagons full of pumpkins
with the words of entire poems carved into them.

There was coffee, but words were the manna from
Heaven sustaining us all.

Once we tasted the gift, we became as radiant as
the golden yellow leaves of the ginkgo tree.

We spread our wings as we make snow angels in
the brilliant sacrifice.

Eternity is in our vision.

—Rita B. Vincent

For your day: *Where do I get my manna from Heaven? What feeds my spirit?*

Day 177

The words below are my memories of a significant dream. I have always prayed to dream of Jesus or Mary. It finally happened in 2009, and when I awoke, I was confused, shocked, afraid, and yet happy. What does it mean? Maybe one day the message in this dream will be fully revealed to me.

My Dream

I am walking in the country, slowly, leisurely.
Not cold, not hot, but comfortable.
It is peaceful.
The wind kicks up
rustling the leaves and the grass.
My senses are keen to something.

I approach the rusted skeleton,
the weeds framing the structure seem like family calling me home.
As if knowing exactly where to go, my feet keep moving,
pulling me deep into the dark arms of my former playground,
the tractor shed
a place where the smell of grease and oil filled lungs
and tools of every shape and size lay in a graveyard of neglect.

As I come closer, I am six years old,
short blonde hair, blue eyes, bare feet – a shy farm girl.
I begin to hear voices: my brother, my father, my uncle.
I hear the clink of tools and the sound of farm equipment.
The dark, cold shed, a place of mystery
a place for men, not little girls.
Then silence.

Rounding the corner, I enter the cold.
To my right is darkness.
A tiny stream of sunlight overhead was all there was.
I feel unsure in the damp murkiness.

I hear something.
My eyes, still blinded by sun, search for the sound, drawing me
closer.
The sound of labored breathing.
Suddenly, without touch, I feel her.
Without sight, I know her.
And then, frozen, I see her bruised feet
the wooden cross claiming her
hiding her
from everyone but me.

I knew in an instant it was her.
Dark hair fell about her gown
I didn't see the nails but they were there.
She was bruised, she was bloody.
I begin to feel my heartbeat.
I hear hers.
I see and smell the leather binding her arms.
She strains to reach out to me.

A cloud passes and the sun filters through the roof once more.
I look up and see her tear-stained face,
her gown wet with agony.
Suddenly, the wind stops.
No more birds
not a sound,
only her breath, her moans and the leather as she strains to free
herself.
Her lips never spoke
only her eyes, brimming with tears,
searching for mine.

No longer six, I stand before her.
Remove me . . . .get me down, her eyes said.
I don't know how, mine replied.
Hopeless, helpless, useless am I.
Her pleading eyes then closed.
Sadly, I don't know what to do.

As I journey from sleep to wakefulness, I lie in bed,
tearful, afraid, unsettled, yet honored.
I really don't know what to feel.
Mary? Was that really you?
What were you trying to tell me?

She was pleading. She was not at peace.
A mother's message delivered and received.

—Jane DeBlieux
For your day: *What powerful messages have you received from dreams? How do you think you should respond to them?*

Day 178

I first used this read/response to Haiku poets with my version of the poet's verse after enjoying the book Between Two Souls by Mary Lou Kownacki. She would read from the poet Ryoken (1758–1831), meditate on the poem, and respond with her own. I too enjoy this practice.

Temple bells die out.
The fragrant blossoms remain.
A perfect evening!
—Basho
Sun has left this day.
Darkness is black and quiet.
Roses on the breeze.
—Avis Lyons LeBlanc

I kill an ant
and realize my three children
have been watching.
—Kato Shuson
Bugs eating my beets
I want to wage war on them.
I know, war is war.
—Avis Lyons LeBlanc

Dewdrop, let me cleanse
in your brief
sweet waters . . .
These dark hands of life
—Basho
Fog sits on field grass.
Wisps float skyward like fingers
and cleanse my thought.
—Avis Lyons LeBlanc

Camellia-petal
fell in silent dawn . . .spilling
a water-jewel

—Basho
Camellia-petal
Dropping pure and white as snow
Covers up green grass.
—Avis Lyons LeBlanc

The lamp once out
Cool stars enter
The window frame.
—Natsume Soseki
My world full of light,
black sky, bright stars often unseen
but I know they shine.
—Avis Lyons LeBlanc

First autumn morning
the mirror I stare into
shows my father's face.
—Murakami Kijo
Where did time get to?
The mirror I stare into
Shows a foreign face.
—Avis Lyons LeBlanc

—Avis Lyons LeBlanc

For your day: *Explore new ways to meditate.*

Day 179

Unless I spend time in the quiet, the language of silence will be an unfamiliar voice to me. I won't hear what my soul is saying until I remove myself from the distractions of noise.

An Unfamiliar Voice

The familiar voices of long ago
were loud, declaring, and demanding:
"You will do this, you will do that."

Today, I bend my ear that
I might hear that which speaks
to me in subtleties.

Like the song of the lark
and music beneath words,
like hearing what
I've never heard before.

I may not be fluent in this language
but there is pull toward it that
I can no longer ignore.

Like a pervading sense of déjà vu
brushing lightly against my skin,
another voice making itself known.

—Wendi Romero

For your day: *May I hear the voice of silence.*

Day 180

I often become a prisoner of my own thoughts and self-proclaimed limitations. I am the one who holds me back.

Emergence

Slave, sleeping in stone,
you rose from the tomb
at dawn. Excess chipped
away, the world can no
longer weigh so heavily
on your head. Prisoner
of the night, you climbed
up from the quarry of life.
From winter to spring,
you mightily emerged.
Your trapped beauty,
alas freed from the grave.
Your time has come—
even the stone can't
hold you back anymore.

—Wendi Romero

For your day: *May I be free from what limits me.*

Day 181

Mystical Glimpses: Notes from My Life

Day 182

Gifts and Giving

Photo by Jill Duhon

Day 183

Now, at last, let me begin to live by faith.
—Thomas Merton

The Kindness of Strangers

Recently I made a trip to France alone to meet a pilgrimage group. On my way back from Europe, I carefully guarded my documents, as I can lose things quite easily. I checked and re-checked my passport, boarding passes and so on.

But on one of the last legs of my trip, from New York to Dallas, I lost my boarding pass. It was marking my place the book I was reading, *I Know Why the Caged Bird Sings,* and I left the book in a food kiosk. I went back but couldn't find it.

I was exhausted from traveling and my heart sank with dread. Airports are filled with angst these days and my body had been picking this up all along the way. I looked at the American counter and it was swamped with passengers for a later flight. My plane was to load in fifteen minutes.

I saw a gentleman in an official looking uniform and asked him if he could help. He replied, "Well, I'm in maintenance, but let me see what I can do." He then walked to the front of the line and motioned to me. The agent there looked at my passport and printed out another boarding pass, handing it to me with a smile.

My eyes filled with tears and I thought, "Why are they being so nice to me? Ah, the kindness of strangers. In big ole New York City. This is what we discover when we travel out of our comfort zones, that kindness is everywhere, that compassion has not died and we have reasons to have faith. We usually don't discover these truths listening to the news or sitting with our friends bemoaning the state of the world; we often have to take ourselves to the edges to discover new reasons for hope.

Dorothy Day, in her famous statement, said that in encountering the poor we must be careful, as we might be entertaining angels unaware. On this day, I was the poor one, and the angels showed up to meet me in my need. My pilgrimage of the heart continued all the way home and long after.

—Lyn Holley Doucet

For your day: *When have I helped a stranger, or been helped by someone I didn't know? What gifts came from this encounter?*

Day 184

If it is encouraging, let him encourage; if it is contributing to the needs of others, let him give generously; if it is leadership, let him govern diligently; if it is showing mercy, let him do it cheerfully. Love must be sincere. Hate what is evil; cling to what is good. Be devoted to one another in brotherly love. Honor one another above yourselves. Never be lacking in zeal, but keep your spiritual fervor, serving the Lord. Be joyful in hope, patient in affliction, faithful in prayer. Share with God's people who are in need. Practice hospitality.
—Romans 12:8-13

The Gift in Caregiving

I'm in prayer this morning, listening to thunder and rain, pondering Paula d'Arcy's words yesterday, "Living the Moment." In caregiving, there are many special moments with my loved ones that will stay in my heart forever, and I'll share just a few.

Caregiving began years ago, but I never thought of it as a gift. I just stepped up and did what I thought I should do for a friend or family member. I thought about what I was doing for them, not the gift they were giving me, until recently.

When I think back about those moments, they continue to show me the power in prayer. Miracles were happening, and I didn't really see them at the time. All these moments and experiences were preparing me for yet another miracle. In caring for loved ones, I have encountered easy days and difficult days. Time flies on those easy days and seems to drag on those difficult ones.

I've had a brother-in-law speak his first words to me after being in a coma for six months. What a moment, hearing "all right" when I asked, "How are you doing today?" as I had every day for months, never giving up hope.

My dad, who suffered more than anyone I had ever seen, with kidney failure, multiple amputations, losing all independence, and becoming incoherent, became lucid, asking questions, four days before passing away. What a moment, when I could answer all his concerns to the best of my ability. This moved him into more acceptance and readiness for the inevitable.

When my step-brother had a major stroke in South Carolina, four months after our dad died, he asked if I would help him. I said yes to my Lord's prompting. After his rehabilitation, he lived in a homeless shelter in Buford, South Carolina for several months. And what a moment, when I picked him up at the train station, in Lafayette, Louisiana. Moving him into his own space, where he has lived now for twelve years, I learned patience and understanding. There are trying times as his health issues continue to decline.

In caring for my mom, since dad died, I am practicing compassion and encouragement. We have our normal arguments, but there is so much more love in our relationship now. She was always there for me, so now I'm there for her. We are having many special moments, sharing issues I never knew about. I'm learning more about her childhood and my own, which makes me more understanding of how God and His love have always been with us, in those dark and light times.

Others call caregiving my gift. I guess I never thought of it as a gift because it comes so easily, most of the time. But as they say, just because it comes easily doesn't mean it's not a gift or your strength. So today, I claim my gift in caregiving, but I also say that their gifts to me are much bigger.

It's not always easy, but I know those trying times won't last forever. I want to bring life to this moment because it is the moment my Lord has given me. Let's wake up to how quickly life is moving. Just think of how many yesterdays have already passed. It blows my mind when

I think about it. So I try to focus less on me, but continue to take care of myself, and love as God loves, unconditionally.

—Denise Broussard

For your day: *Can you think of someone who might need your care? If you are already a caregiver, think of those special moments shared with your loved ones.*

Day 185

Opening my heart to the blessings of my limitations can help me see Your wisdom, O Holy Mystery. When I can be open, share my feelings of inadequacy or talent, I am more likely to recognize the flow of Love in which I am living. I wrote this poem-sketch at a group gathering in which I was feeling very unable to accomplish the creative task we were invited to do. I shared my frustration with the group, and this was the example that helped one other person in that group to reach out.

This writing method, called poem-sketching, begins with listing four words, pondering those words for several minutes, and allowing them to be arranged in phrases or sentences, as I am urged by the meaning they have for me at this moment. A more complete description of this process is found in Sandford Lyne's book, *Writing Poetry from the Inside Out.*

Within   **Share**   **Community**   **Gift**
I may never know which gift in me is given
so when I share it;
it reaches its real purpose.
It can be my flaws or one of my talents
in my judgment.
The treasury of gifts within multiply when,
without my directing them,
they create community.

—Betty Landreneau

For your day: *Let me see my talents and limitations with Your love, O God.*

Day 186

A Letter to My Husband

A friend gifted me with a precious Hallmark book entitled *If Only I Knew* by Lance Wubbels. The cover also read, "Gentle reminders to help you treasure the people in your life." This inspired me to write a letter to my husband to express my love for him.

None of us know how long the people we love and admire will be in our lives, nor do we know how long we will have to tell them how much we love and appreciate them. I was led to write this letter to you before it is too late to do so. Often, I find it is easier to find a card that expresses what I want to say, but not this time. I want to tell you how deeply I love you.

As we maneuver through the conditions of our life together, I sometimes think you might be just "putting up with me." I realize that you don't see life with me in this way. You have told me over and over that you love me since our second date! If I painted a portrait of you, I'd have to paint the twinkle in your blue-green eyes that you say I put there. I'd have to paint the smile on your face that encourages me when I'm hurting or when I have to release something that I cannot handle. I'd have to paint you sweetly pinching me or giving me some kind of love tap that tells me that I am the only one God made for you. I'd have to find a way to paint how we enjoy each other's company and how exasperated I am when we waste time arguing or fretting about the future (mostly me). I'd have to paint you with our children and their spouses and our grandchildren being so gentle, taking your time, playing games with them, supporting them with your compliments, or with your very last dime. I'd have to include the tenderness with which you explain things to them or how you gently hold the little ones' hands. I'd have to paint the tears you shed when rebellion was part of our lives, but then I'd capture the joy in your step as you walked our daughter down the aisle or the excitement on your face at the baseball park when our son pitched years ago and again today as you watch our grandson do the same.

I'd also have to paint you conscientious about providing for me since we have been married and not losing hope when times were rough. You smile when you go to work. Not to get away but because you genuinely like people and you are proud to work hard for us. After all, you have been working since you were ten years old when you were a shoe shine boy. I could go on and on, but I don't think I could do this portrait justice – this portrait of the best husband, friend and most loving man in my world. I will love you always!

—Cheryl Delahoussaye

For your day: *Tell someone you love how much it means to you to have them in your life.*

Day 187

Unexpected Gifts, Rivers Turning

At the last moment, there was a change of leader,
But our hearts were resolved to yield to whatever we were to receive.
We came together at the river's turning, seeking to find a clearer path to the
Source of our being.
Each one had her own agenda, yet once we began seeking,
they all seemed to melt into one.
We were comforted by the gentle breezes under the massive oaks dripping with moss.
The wind art reflected the constant movement within our hearts and thoughts.
As we continued to seek the deeper meaning of "what is," we walked the labyrinth, passing one another on the journey, honoring the silence, rejoicing in the moment.
Unfamiliar faces faded, and familiar souls emerged.
Filters dissolved, hearts united, and the river continued its journey.

—Pat Low

For your day: *How can I move forward with confidence, even when I don't know where the flow will take me?*

Day 188

Gifts and Giving: Notes from My Life

Day 189

God Is Love Loving

Day 190

Everyone just wants to be loved. If they can't find love, they make war.
—Lyn Holley Doucet

Like many authors who read constantly, I can't say if I created this quote; I think I did. It came from prayer one day as I pondered my own heart. Many others have said the same, that love is what we are seeking. We have all sorts of dysfunctional ways of getting love: we compete, we strive, we put others down to make ourselves greater, we nurse our angers because they make us feel stronger. And yes, look around, we make wars, large and small.

It is hard to understand that we *are* the love we seek. That we are love incarnate, that love can come through us in a constant stream. When Jesus commanded us to love one another as ourselves, he must have believed that we had everything we needed to do so. The ego within always wants more, more, more. But it is only through shedding—our false selves, our ego strivings, our needs to be special—that we can truly love. It's the hardest and the easiest thing. We just need to see in a brand-new way. I receive love when I give love, authentically and freely, no holding back.

For a while, I was collecting cicada shells. I found them on the door of the cabin, the sidewalk, all the places I frequented. They spoke to me of transformation. The cicada burrows in the ground for many years until she surfaces, sheds her carapace, and sings her song for a season. Many of us wear carapaces, we are protecting ourselves from more hurt, rejection, or disappointment. But we must become tender, we must shed our old skins in order to sing the one song we have been freely given. It's a love song, and it's the only melody that really matters.

—Lyn Holley Doucet

For your day: *I will open my heart to love.*

Day 191

Christ has indeed been raised from the dead. So in Him all will be made alive.
—I Corinthians 15:20

Lenten Time!

I was working outside one gorgeous day just before Easter. The trees were shedding their leaves. Flowers were starting to bloom. I found lifeless and rotting wood hidden under leaves. Birthing and dying, nature does it and so do we.

I find myself anticipating Good Friday and Easter. Life and death, pain and suffering, to joy and love, have all been happening since the beginning. So, as I think of Easter, a dogwood tree comes to my mind. No, I don't have one, but I think about where I could plant one.

The legend I've read at Easter time is that, when dogwoods flower, Christ caused the flowers to be a reminder of the cross. The flower has two long and two short petals, and it has what looks like nail prints to remind us that Christ suffered on the cross with nails through His hands.

"The petals shall have blood stains marked brown / and in the blossom's center a thorny crown. / All who see it will think of me, / nailed to a cross from a dogwood tree. / Protected and cherished this tree shall be. / A reflection to all of my agony." (*Author unknown*)

Pink dogwood blushes with shame. Weeping dogwood symbolizes sorrow. Red dogwood reminds us of bloodshed. Life is such mystery. I like the idea that God has placed so many reminders on earth and in the sky; they cause us to glorify and praise Him for His greatness, mercy, love, and indescribable gift.

But the miracle of His Resurrection is where we focus our energy and our love. We must never forget that God so loved the world. He gave His only Son for us to have eternal life.

—Denise Broussard

For your day: *Where do you see reminders left by God for you?*

Day 192

I planted, Apollos watered, but God caused the growth. Therefore neither the one who plants nor the one who waters is anything, but only God who causes the growth. Each will receive wages in proportion to their labor...for we are God's co-workers.
—1 Corinthians 3:6-9

I have often wondered how God weaved godself into my mom's psyche, heart, and soul. She liked learning about scripture, but she did not share with me her relationship or conversation with God. She went to Mass, yet never seemed to me to be visibly inspired by the celebration. I wonder if the language of liturgy and faith sharing was perhaps foreign to her. Perhaps having lived apart from her further blurred my listening.

Yet on this last visit in April 2016, it became clear to me that, in her twilight years, Mom probably feels most loved and receptive to love through her flowers and garden, especially her confederate jasmine, her signature beauty. She has several, and you can almost smell their ethereal scent in a photo. Mostly I see my mom's eyes and heart sparkle when spring bursts forth in bloom. She has other favorites like the "chismes," periwinkles, ferns, and the bright yellow blooms of the Esperanza. The lush greenness of the augustine grass fills her with pride, too, as did the "mayitos" that she and my grandmother planted. I cringe when I see her bend over to pull weeds as she sits untethered in her motorized scooter. I marvel at her enthusiasm to be outside in the heat of the afternoon or the morning's cool air. My heart smiles with gladness that in her lawn, garden, and yard space, joy and patience bloom in my mom.She guided the creation of this lush green space through the years, adding a plant here, some mulch there, a bench, an edging, stepping stones, an arbor for the confederate jasmine in the front yard, a family glider gifted to her from her brother, Oscar. Of course, a yard in Laredo must have a bougainvillea. Perhaps implementing the creation of the yardscape was where she most felt like a divine handmaiden: focused, consumed, and in union with a rhythm greater than herself that carried the vision through her into fulfillment. It's as if what she brought into bloom is what is most upholding her well-being at age 81; now that she is mostly confined to sitting in her scooter.

She mentioned to me how infuriated she gets when my dad scolds her for being outside for long hours, especially alone. He fears she will get hurt and probably gets annoyed that he needs to be the watchman, awake and on alert until the sitter or one of my brothers arrives. He prefers being inside sleeping, walking the hallway, or watching TV for hours, which equally annoys her. Now I realize that chiding her and telling her to come inside takes her away from her experience of heaven, of unity with a deeper, authentic self where she knows who she is and what she believes to be true. It is as if the beauty of what she participates in creating beckons her and woos her to remain in the garden.

I had worried that my mom may not have experienced a divine sheltering presence in this life that would help her transition when she passes into her journey after death. I discovered that her soul has been weaving itself into this sacred relationship without being tethered to many spoken or written "holy" words. This knowing eases my angst. Her path will be lined and laced with lush vegetation and blooms of confederate jasmine welcoming her home.

—Elsa Diana Mendoza

For your day: *How have you participated in creating something beautiful, with the understanding that the expression of beauty is infinite?*

Day 193

Letter from God

When I am struggling to find self-acceptance, I think about the letter that I imagined God wrote to me.

Cheryl,

I love you. It is as simple as that! I love you. You are my child. The daughter whom I created. You are my beloved.

You are my Cher'. Even your name bears this name that means my beloved.

You struggle so much sometimes. Don't wonder if you are doing things right. Just love as you have been told by the Scriptures.

Don't make your loved ones the center of your worship. Put me first. I have told you this in church, in dreams and through your loved ones' words.

Before bed when your husband reads to you from devotionals, listen to the words that tell you of my love and how much I want you to spend time with me. When I touch your heart with words like, "Do not be afraid! Stay calm! Be grateful! Be kind and generous! Love others!" Listen to ME! Just listen! I might say, "Ask for my forgiveness and forgive others." Listen.

My voice is the one I want you to recognize. When you hear voices from your past, you pull forward so many negatives, so many hurts. When you see yourself doing this, make your thoughts positive. Remember I was there with you and loved you then. If voices from the future speak of worry, know that I am there with you to diminish your fears! I am positive, healing love. I know that sometimes you feel as though you have not accomplished much, that you have lived your life and everything is downhill from here. You heard once that hurting people hurt others and you don't want to do this. Don't listen to those voices that frighten you, discourage you and pester you that you are not good. So much more awaits you! Open your heart to my love. Let me bind your wounds and heal all of you – your heart, your mind, and your soul. You will receive my abundance and my grace-filled guidance as I have promised to provide. Can you understand how much I love My Cheryl? I do. It's as simple as that!

—Cheryl Delahoussaye

For your day: *Sit a while longer and contemplate God's love for you. Consider writing your thoughts after.*

Day 194

You were born with potential. You were born with goodness and trust. You were born with ideals and dreams. You were born with greatness. You were born with wings. You are not meant for crawling, so don't. You have wings. Learn to use them and fly.
—Rumi

Finding Wings

I discover my wings
as I gaze upon yours.
Only when I recognize your greatness and beauty
do I see my own.
Striving for flight leaves me stranded on the cliff of longing.
Dreams, serenely pondered,
embrace the gift of agreement.
I agree to offer my vulnerability
by telling you my heart.
I agree to reverence your vulnerability
and to honor all our possibilities.
Together, our wings gain flight,
our potential magnifies by more
than the sum of its parts.

—Avis Lyons LeBlanc

For your day: *Recognize your own potential for greatness when you see that trait in others.*

Day 195

God Is Love Loving: Notes from My Life

Day 196

I wrote this shortly after attending the Hildegard of Bingen retreat. I felt such an intense "power" that was held within the circle. I felt the power of the feminine and felt then—and to this day—that, as a community of women, we really cannot fathom the great things we are capable of. We need to be bold and brave.

Art by Dana Manly

"You complete our circle—this melting pot of she,
a natural reflection of love, acceptance and compassion,
a oneness like no other. You know our power, but do we?"

—Jane DeBlieux

Printed in the United States
By Bookmasters